Russian History: A Very Short Introduction

VERY SHORT INTRODUCTIONS are for anyone wanting a stimulating and accessible way in to a new subject. They are written by experts, and have been published in more than 25 languages worldwide.

The series began in 1995, and now represents a wide variety of topics in history, philosophy, religion, science, and the humanities. The VSI library now contains 300 volumes—a Very Short Introduction to everything from ancient Egypt and Indian philosophy to conceptual art and cosmology—and will continue to grow in a variety of disciplines.

Very Short Introductions available now:

ADVERTISING Winston Fletcher
AFRICAN HISTORY John Parker and
   Richard Rathbone
AGNOSTICISM Robin Le Poidevin
AMERICAN IMMIGRATION
   David A. Gerber
AMERICAN POLITICAL PARTIES
   AND ELECTIONS L. Sandy Maisel
THE AMERICAN PRESIDENCY
   Charles O. Jones
ANARCHISM Colin Ward
ANCIENT EGYPT Ian Shaw
ANCIENT GREECE Paul Cartledge
ANCIENT PHILOSOPHY Julia Annas
ANCIENT WARFARE
   Harry Sidebottom
ANGELS David Albert Jones
ANGLICANISM Mark Chapman
THE ANGLO-SAXON AGE John Blair
THE ANIMAL KINGDOM
   Peter Holland
ANIMAL RIGHTS David DeGrazia
ANTISEMITISM Steven Beller
THE APOCRYPHAL GOSPELS
   Paul Foster
ARCHAEOLOGY Paul Bahn
ARCHITECTURE Andrew Ballantyne
ARISTOCRACY William Doyle
ARISTOTLE Jonathan Barnes
ART HISTORY Dana Arnold
ART THEORY Cynthia Freeland
ATHEISM Julian Baggini
AUGUSTINE Henry Chadwick
AUTISM Uta Frith

THE AZTECS David Carrasco
BARTHES Jonathan Culler
BEAUTY Roger Scruton
BESTSELLERS John Sutherland
THE BIBLE John Riches
BIBLICAL ARCHAEOLOGY
   Eric H. Cline
BIOGRAPHY Hermione Lee
THE BLUES Elijah Wald
THE BOOK OF MORMON
   Terryl Givens
THE BRAIN Michael O'Shea
BRITISH POLITICS Anthony Wright
BUDDHA Michael Carrithers
BUDDHISM Damien Keown
BUDDHIST ETHICS Damien Keown
CANCER Nicholas James
CAPITALISM James Fulcher
CATHOLICISM Gerald O'Collins
THE CELL Terence Allen and
   Graham Cowling
THE CELTS Barry Cunliffe
CHAOS Leonard Smith
CHILDREN'S LITERATURE
   Kimberley Reynolds
CHINESE LITERATURE
   Sabina Knight
CHOICE THEORY Michael Allingham
CHRISTIAN ART Beth Williamson
CHRISTIAN ETHICS D. Stephen Long
CHRISTIANITY Linda Woodhead
CITIZENSHIP Richard Bellamy
CLASSICAL MYTHOLOGY
   Helen Morales

Available soon:

For more information visit our website
www.oup.com/vsi/

Geoffrey Hosking

RUSSIAN HISTORY

A Very Short Introduction

OXFORD
UNIVERSITY PRESS

OXFORD

UNIVERSITY PRESS

Great Clarendon Street, Oxford OX2 6DP

Oxford University Press is a department of the University of Oxford.
It furthers the University's objective of excellence in research, scholarship,
and education by publishing worldwide in

Oxford New York

Auckland Cape Town Dar es Salaam Hong Kong Karachi
Kuala Lumpur Madrid Melbourne Mexico City Nairobi
New Delhi Shanghai Taipei Toronto

With offices in

Argentina Austria Brazil Chile Czech Republic France Greece
Guatemala Hungary Italy Japan Poland Portugal Singapore
South Korea Switzerland Thailand Turkey Ukraine Vietnam

Oxford is a registered trade mark of Oxford University Press
in the UK and in certain other countries

Published in the United States
by Oxford University Press Inc., New York

British Library Cataloguing in Publication Data

Data available

Library of Congress Cataloging in Publication Data

Data available

Typeset by SPI Publisher Services, Pondicherry, India
Printed in Great Britain on acid-free paper by
Ashford Colour Press Ltd, Gosport, Hampshire

ISBN: 978-0-19-958098-9

1 3 5 7 9 10 8 6 4 2

Contents

Preface

I am grateful to the students and colleagues who have helped me develop and clarify my thoughts during forty years of teaching Russian history, and especially to Roger Bartlett, John Gooding, and Martin Sixsmith, who commented on an earlier version of this text. Mistakes and misconceptions remain, of course, my own.

List of illustrations

Introduction

In Thomas Mann's novel *The Magic Mountain*, which is a kind of panorama of pre-First World War European civilization, there are, appropriately enough, quite a number of Russian characters. They sit at two separate tables: the Good Russian table and the Bad Russian table. Our thinking about Russia today has not advanced much beyond these facile labels. At one table, we seat Tolstoy, Tchaikovsky, Repin and Sakharov; at the other, most of the Tsars, Stalin, and nowadays often Putin. We seem unable to approach Russia without a strong moral and emotional input, positive or negative. It is in many ways a European country, yet it is too large, too close to us, and too strange to fit into any comfortable pigeonholes.

In fact, the Good Russia and the Bad Russia are indissolubly linked by the arduous and challenging task of building a coherent polity on the flat open plains of northern Eurasia, then defending it against all comers, including the more developed states of Europe lying immediately to the west. Of all the great gunpowder empires of Eurasia, Russia proved the most durable. It has been a remarkable success story, yet one which had its own weaknesses programmed into it. It rested on a tacit compact between ruler, elites, and communities of ordinary people, renewed after periods of upheaval and crisis, yet never wholly harmonious, always subject to internal strains.

That uneasy relationship is my central story, from its origin in Muscovy right through to its re-embodiment in post-Soviet Russia. Throughout, I have tried to give as much attention to local communities as to the elites and the ruler. First, though, we must look at the prelude, in the very different history of Kievan Rus.

Chapter 1
Kievan Rus and the Mongols

In 1237, Mongol invaders attacked the town of Suzdal.

> They plundered the Church of the Holy Virgin and burned down
> the prince's court and burned down the Monastery of St Dmitrii,
> and the others they plundered. The old monks and nuns and priests
> and the blind, lame, hunchbacked and sick they killed, and the
> young monks and nuns and priests and priests' wives and deacons
> and deacons' wives, and their daughters and sons – all were led
> away into captivity.

Such images have haunted the minds of Russians over the
centuries. They have been re-enacted within living memory in the
German invasion of 1941. Whatever else they may have wanted,
Russians have always longed for security from terrifying and
murderous assaults across the flat open frontiers to east and west.
They could not have that security, though, without restraining the
feuding of their own internal strongmen. That was the need which
motivated the creation of the first Rus state, more than three
centuries earlier. The *Primary Chronicle*, the first East Slav
foundation narrative, reported of the 9th-century Slav tribes that

> there was no law among them, but tribe rose against tribe.
> Discord thus ensued, and they began to war against one
> another....Accordingly they went overseas to the Varangian Russes.

[And they] said to the people of Rus 'Our whole land is great and rich, but there is no order in it. Come to rule and reign over us.'

Probably this was not a single event but a gradual process by which scattered tribes accepted Varangian, or Viking, rule in the interests of peace, security, and stable commerce. The Vikings established fortified urban settlements on the trading route from Scandinavia to Byzantium along the rivers Volkhov, Dvina, and Dnieper. At the southernmost of these settlements, Kiev, they established a capital city from where their *kagan* (later Great Prince) could enforce his authority over unruly tribes. It forms the birthplace of two of today's sovereign states, Russia and Ukraine. Around Kiev they built a semi-circle of fortresses to defend it against nomadic raids. They intermingled readily with their subjects and adopted their tongue, so that a common East Slav language and culture emerged, albeit one with a marked social hierarchy: the prince and his *druzhina* (armed henchmen) formed the elite.

This fixing of authority and culture made life safer and more prosperous: a lively commerce and settled agriculture developed. Kinship faded as the basic principle of social organization, and the names of tribes disappeared from the Chronicles, to be replaced by urban and village communities. The princes awarded their warriors the right of *kormlenie*, that is to be supported (literally: fed) by local communities in return for guaranteeing protection. This was a variant of the 'gift economy'; it gave local communities a means to get to know their masters, gauge their reactions, and establish – or sometimes not – some mutual trust and a give-and-take relationship with them.

To regulate their own affairs, village communities had their own assemblies, for which the term *mir*, meaning peace or harmony, gradually came into use. The urban assemblies were known as *veche*: only their support or 'acclamation' rendered a prince's authority fully legitimate. All male citizens were members of the *veche*, and they had both the right and duty to take up arms in defence of the community.

Establishing a unified kingdom, however, proved more difficult. The various sons of the Kievan Great Prince regularly fought one another for the succession. Efforts to curtail these feuds resembled those of Charlemagne's successors, who were also trying to suppress lesser princes and unruly tribes. The best way to establish law and order and to generate mutual solidarity was to accept a monotheistic religion. That is what Prince Vladimir (r. 978–1015) did in 988 by accepting the Byzantine form of Christianity. It offered attractive assets to a prince seeking to consolidate his authority: it condemned blood feuds and it justified the princely imposition of law, order, and peace. Two of its first saints, Boris and Gleb, sons of Vladimir, were said to have been murdered by rivals because they declined to participate in dynastic feuds. As it extended its network of parishes, the church also provided the most effective way of disseminating both moral concepts and observance of the law.

A close relationship with Byzantium was especially beneficial to a people who already traded with it. Orthodox Christianity had other advantages: it accepted partnership with secular authority, and its liturgy was conducted in a language akin to the vernacular, so that it was closer to the people than Latin Christianity. On the other hand, after the Byzantine and Roman churches split apart in the 11th century, Orthodoxy lost its ecumenical contact with much of Central and Western Europe.

To coordinate the sinews of authority, Vladimir dispersed his sons to various regional bases within his realm. Each had a *druzhina*, entitled to *kormlenie* from local communities. Vladimir's work of consolidation was continued by his son, Iaroslav (r. 1019–54), who rebuilt Kiev as an imposing capital city, with stone fortifications, its own Cathedral of St Sophia, named after Byzantium's principal church, and a Golden Gate for ceremonial entry. The Kievan Caves Monastery became a centre of Christian learning and culture, and over several decades in the 11th and early 12th centuries, it produced the *Primary Chronicle*, which identified the Kievan realm as the joint enterprise of Vladimir's Riurikovich dynasty (called after the first Varangian prince, Riurik). Iaroslav promulgated the first Rus-ian law code, the *Russkaia Pravda. Pravda* is a key word for understanding Russian culture: it means not only truth, but also justice and what is right according to God's law. The code's main contribution was to severely restrict blood feud and supplant it with a closely calibrated scheme of fines for murder, injury, insult, or violation of property. The capacity to impose such fines presupposed both strong central authority and a stable monetary system.

At the northern end of the trading route from Scandinavia to Byzantium, the city of Novgorod developed as a major economic centre. It gained control over the immense territories of the far north and east, and it enforced tribute on the local Baltic and Finno-Ugrian peoples. From the huge forests, the Novgorodians

1. The Caves Monastery, Kiev

could sell timber, furs, wax, and honey both southwards to Kiev and Byzantium, and westwards to the Baltic and Germany through the Hanseatic League. It had its own Cathedral of St Sophia and its own archbishop, who was second only to the Kiev Metropolitan. Its *veche* was especially influential and frequently reasserted its right to elect its own prince, whatever the dynastic arrangements laid down from Kiev.

Iaroslav did his best to ensure strong collective leadership by regularizing the succession to the princely thrones, not in direct succession from father to son, but passing through the younger brothers according to seniority. This was to establish the principle that the realm was a kind of federation belonging to the princely family as a whole, while also removing the grounds for feuds within that family. The oldest living brother was to supervise the whole arrangement.

Collective rule was honoured in principle, but proved too difficult to manage in practice. After Iaroslav's death, his brothers and cousins periodically fought each other over the inheritance, yet at times they had to curtail their feuds to face common threats from the nomadic horsemen of the steppe. During the especially alarming raids of the Kipchaks (or Polovtsy) in the 1090s, the princes met and renewed their dynastic agreement. It was successful in coping with the immediate danger, and gave Kievan Rus another generation of peace, but it did not prove durable.

In 1113, the citizens of Kiev invited Vladimir of Pereiaslavl, the most successful commander against the Kipchaks, to rule over them as Great Prince. After his victories, he received from Byzantium a fur-lined crown, the 'Monomakh crown', as a symbol of his God-given authority. He was a thoughtful and pious but also practical ruler, who believed in taking personal responsibility for all the major burdens of princely authority: war, the dynasty and its household, justice, charity and patronage, and the observance of *pravda*. He outlined his

5

precepts in a written *Exhortation* (*Pouchenie*) to his sons, urging them to rule not only through military means, but also through 'repentance, tears, and almsgiving'. This combination of physical power with Christian morality continued to be an ideal for the rulers of Rus/Russia.

After Vladimir's death, the fragmentation of Kievan Rus resumed. This happened partly because it was growing in size and prosperity. Trade was bringing economic activity to new areas, especially to the north and east, where there was abundant timber, furs and fish, and tree cover offered better protection against steppe raiders. New towns were founded and junior princes used them as bases for securing their own authority; in particular Vladimir, Suzdal, and Rostov became wealthy commercial centres, though as yet not serious rivals of Kiev and Novgorod. New churches were built and new bishoprics created under the aegis of the Kiev Metropolitan. At the same time, the princes' feuding over land and succession rights repeatedly undermined these promising developments.

Mongol overlordship

In the early 13th century another, much more serious, danger emerged. Under the Mongol tribe, a new kind of steppe federation was being created, with its centre between Lake Baikal and the Great Wall of China. It created large, extremely mobile, and proficient cavalry armies, which conquered China under Chingis Khan. They then moved westwards, integrating the scattered nomadic tribes of Central Eurasia, among them the Kipchaks. Here the Rus princes' disunity proved fatal. When the army of Batu, Chingis Khan's grandson, approached Riazan in 1237, the princes were engaged in ferocious battles for control of Kiev, and did not respond to Riazan's appeal for help. Over the next three years, Batu's cavalry was able to attack cities singly, without ever facing a combined Rus army, inflicting the carnage we saw above.

In each case, his men looted, destroyed, and killed without mercy. Many towns lost most of their population; able-bodied survivors were deported to slavery or to service in Batu's army.

Eventually Batu withdrew, concluding that direct occupation of such unfamiliar forested territory was beyond him. He set up the capital of his domain (*ulus*), usually called by historians the Golden Horde, at Sarai on the lower Volga. From there, he and his successors fashioned a system of dominion over the Rus principalities. They awarded each ruling prince a *iarlyk* (the right to rule), after a symbolic ceremony of submission. In selecting a successor for each principality, the Golden Horde followed wherever possible the established Kievan principles – but kept the final decision in their own hands. They appointed to each prince a Mongol tribute-collector and a viceroy, who carried out a census of the local population – an indication of a highly developed administrative system – to ensure that the people paid tribute to Sarai and contributed recruits to a militia or to a forced labour brigade.

Traditionally, Russians have regarded the Mongol overlordship as an unmitigated disaster. Recent research suggests, however, that, after the initial shock and destruction, it had compensations, even though for several generations it imposed a heavy burden on the Rus population, against which townsfolk periodically rebelled. The Mongols restrained princely feuding. They built and maintained a network of communications, together with postal relay stations, superior to anything that had existed in Kiev. Through it, they plugged Rus into a Central Asian trading network which extended to China, the world's wealthiest civilization. This trade laid the basis for an economic recovery which gathered pace during the 14th century. The princes who cooperated with the Mongols did especially well: their authority was guaranteed, and they received Mongol support against any rebellion in their territories.

For the Orthodox Church, the Mongol dominion was almost a golden age. The Mongols were on principle tolerant in religious matters, and later themselves became Muslims. They granted the church immunity from tribute and from the obligation to deliver recruits for military and labour service. It was able to accumulate extensive landholdings and vassals. Much of the work of opening up new territories was accomplished by monasteries, which thus became nurseries of both spiritual and economic power. Moreover, with the fragmentation and subjugation of secular authority, the church was the only institution able to speak for Rus as a whole. The Kiev Metropolitan regarded himself as the custodian of its integrity: he took the title Metropolitan of All Rus, and spent much of his time travelling round the various dioceses.

Meanwhile, Novgorod was going its own way. Its far north-western forest location deterred the Mongols from attacking it. Its prince, Alexander (r. 1236–63), negotiated skilfully with them, and in return for paying an ample tribute received a special charter guaranteeing the city's right to govern itself. He had good reason to mollify the Mongols, for his western frontier was threatened by the Swedes; he defeated them in 1240 in a battle on the River Neva – hence his nickname Nevskii. In addition, the Teutonic Knights were trying to block Novgorod's lucrative trading routes in the Baltic. When they advanced towards the city itself in 1242, Alexander overcame them in battle on the frozen Lake Peipus. The scale of the battle may have been exaggerated by later chroniclers, but its significance cannot be. It established the River Narva and Lake Peipus as a permanent boundary between Eastern and Western Christianity.

Alexander's younger son, Daniil, became ruler of the new principality of Moscow. During the early 14th century, he and his successors succeeded in establishing themselves as the favoured recipients of the *iarlyk* of Great Prince, even though, as scions of a cadet Riurikovich line, they did not qualify under the Kievan succession rules. Daniil's son, Ivan I (Ivan Kalita, or 'moneybags',

r. 1325–41), received the *iarlyk* in 1328, having seen off a rival from Tver. He practised unswerving loyalty to the Golden Horde, and used his function as their tribute-gatherer to enrich his own principality. By subsidizing neighbouring princes, he was able to attract their support and that of their trading towns, and in some cases actually integrate their territories into his own. Gradually, Moscow ceased to observe the Kievan dynastic rules and went over to straightforward patrimonial succession, from father to eldest son. The importance of doing so was underlined when in 1425, on the death of Vasilii I, his brother contested the succession of his son, and plunged Muscovy into a civil war which lasted nearly thirty years. Later princes and their boyars (leading warriors) were determined to prevent any repetition of this disaster.

The recovery of Rus took place not only in the north and east. The south-western principalities, notably Galicia and Volynia, allied themselves with Lithuania, which defeated the Golden Horde at the Battle of Blue Waters in 1362, and was able to establish its authority over Kiev and most of the original heartland of Rus. From the late 14th century, Lithuania, for its own protection, sought union with Poland, to form what at the time was the largest kingdom in Europe. The Lithuanian princes accepted the Catholic religion, though many of their people remained Orthodox. In this way, the western and south-western principalities of Kievan Rus adopted an elite Latinate Polish culture, which distinguished them from those of the north and east. The language spoken in the west, initially known as Rusin (Ruthenian), evolved into modern Belorussian and Ukrainian. Eventually, their territories became contemporary Belorussia and a large part of Ukraine.

Since the Metropolitanate was the most important 'all-Rus' institution, its location and powers were vital to the development of Kievan Rus's successor states. Kiev itself lost its ascendancy because it was especially vulnerable to steppe raids. In 1325, the

Metropolitanate relocated to Moscow; Metropolitan Petr, who made the move, was subsequently canonized with the support of Ivan Kalita, and his tomb became a pilgrimage site. This was a crucial moment: from then on, Moscow became the centre of Russian Orthodox Christianity, though at times contested by Kievan Metropolitans with Lithuanian backing.

During the 14th and 15th centuries, monasteries multiplied and acquired extensive new lands in the northern and eastern forests. Their motive was both spiritual and economic. When young monks became discontented with the discipline in their home foundations, they would break away to set up their own *skit* (hermitage) further into the forest, where to achieve spiritual concentration they could be alone or share divine worship with just a few like-minded colleagues. In the course of time, other devotees would join them, build their own huts or shelters close by, and so a whole new monastery would appear. The most skilled and experienced monks became revered elders (*startsy*), whose spiritual counsel was sought by believers from all ranks of society. Dostoevsky depicted one as Father Zosima in his *Brothers Karamazov*.

Such was the biography of St Sergy of Radonezh, who left home with his brother and built a chapel deep in the forest. He acquired a reputation for spiritual insight, and gradually other monks and seekers joined him. Eventually, they set up a full-scale monastery, of which they invited him to become the abbot. Reluctantly, and only on the insistence of the local bishop, he agreed. His foundation later became the Lavra of the Holy Trinity and St Sergy, future site of the Moscow Patriarchate and centre of Russian Orthodoxy.

The search for spiritual peace and concentration also inspired icon painters associated with the Moscow princely court and the Trinity Lavra. Feofan the Greek and his pupil, Andrei Rublev, developed Byzantine iconic models, making their figures less monumental, more graceful and expressive in their gestures and appearance. Rublev's Trinity is perhaps the best known of all Orthodox icons: its light blue colouring, the meek and trusting way the three angelic figures respond to each other, express the spiritual peace and mutual communion (later known as *sobornost*) which has remained an ideal for Russian believers.

2. Andrei Rublev's icon of the Holy Trinity

3. An iconostasis in the Moscow Kremlin

The decline of the Golden Horde and the rise of Muscovy

The very wealth of the Golden Horde, based on Eurasian commerce, encouraged its subordinate rulers to utilize their *ulus* as centres of settled prosperity and independent power. In the 1370s, one such warlord, Timur (or Tamerlane), carved out a Central Asian empire, the last of the great nomadic super-states. One of his generals, Mamai, set up his own independent khanate west of the Volga and claimed the whole of Rus as his *ulus*. The princes of Rus were faced with two sets of demands for tribute, but also with the opportunity to take advantage of their overlords' conflicts. In order to overcome the growing power of Moscow, Mamai allied himself with Lithuania. Moscow had always deliberately avoided armed conflict with the Horde. In 1380, though, when Mamai moved on Moscow, Prince Dmitry, fortified (as legend has it) by the formal blessing of Sergy, decided to challenge him on the field of Kulikovo, on the upper River Don. Dmitry's army succeeded in repelling the Mongol cavalry charges before Mamai's Lithuanian allies could arrive. Dmitry became known as Dmitry Donskoi in honour of his victory.

The Mongols' yoke was shaken but not overthrown. They decided to demonstrate who was master and raided Moscow two years later. Dmitry meekly accepted the *iarlyk* again. All the same, unquestioning acceptance of Mongol domination had faltered. Moscow had become the undoubted leader among the north-eastern principalities. Over the next two generations, a series of writers of chronicles and narrative poems began to extol Moscow as the leader of the forces of Christendom against the Muslims. In this narrative, Kulikovo and Sergy's blessing occupied central place; Dmitry Donskoi became the saintly prince who with God's help had delivered victory over the infidels. By the same token, the 'land of Rus' became identified with the power of the Muscovite

Great Prince. This was the launch of Moscow's fusion of strong state power with religious mission.

Despite the legend, Moscow had augmented its power and prestige not by opposing the Mongols but by cultivating good relations with them, proving themselves reliable tribute-payers and upholders of order. In the course of that experience, they learned much about the art of government: how to conduct a census and use it for taxation purposes, how to raise an army, maintain rapid communications over extensive territory, and exploit trade whilst also extracting dues from it. The steppe khans ruled by intermittent consultation with their leading warriors when important decisions had to be taken. The Muscovite Great Prince likewise summoned his boyars to periodical gatherings which historians have called the Boyar Duma. He issued major decrees with the wording 'the boyars advised and the Great Prince resolved...'.

Concentrating power and gaining the consensus of the junior princes and boyars became the paramount priority for the Great Princes, especially after the mid-15th-century civil war showed how dangerous disunity was. Their success enabled Moscow to become the largest and most flourishing of the post-Kievan principalities, with the single exception of Novgorod. Between 1462 and 1533, Muscovy roughly tripled in size and population. By persuasion, marriage settlement, and the occasional threat of war, Moscow brought under its sway several principalities of the north and east. The largest prize was Novgorod itself, which was trying to form an alliance with Lithuania in order to maintain its independence and commercial links with the Baltic. In 1478, Ivan III (r. 1462–1505) marched into the city, closed the *veche*, and took down its summoning bell, symbol of its independence. He deported many of Novgorod's landowners and awarded their extensive lands as *pomestia* (service estates) to his own followers. In the following decades, making such awards from newly acquired land enabled the Muscovite Great Prince to create his own army, with its commanders answerable to him. Junior princes had to take their place in the boyar hierarchy.

Up until the late 15th century, all the same, Moscow still had a nominal overlord, the Khan of the Great Horde, one of the remnants of the defunct Golden Horde. In practice, Ivan III, though he continued to pay tribute, ignored his theoretical obligation to seek consent for his policies from the Khan. In 1480, Khan Akhmet made one final attempt to enforce this obligation by moving his armies towards Moscow. Ivan barred his way on the River Ugra, and after a long standoff, Akhmet retreated. This was a tacit acknowledgement that Mongol suzerainty was no longer enforceable, though Moscow continued to pay tribute for a few more years.

At around the same period, the church was also emerging from under the canopy of Byzantium. As the Byzantine Empire became progressively weaker, more of its worldly responsibilities devolved upon the Patriarch, who reacted by attempting a reunion with Rome. At the Council of Ferrara-Florence (1438–9), the Orthodox accepted the demands of the Vatican on all essential doctrinal matters. Metropolitan Isidor, who attended on behalf of Muscovy, signed the concluding document, and returned home a Roman cardinal. He entered the city in solemn procession holding aloft a crucifix, but to his horror was arrested and confined in a monastery for apostasy. Henceforth, the Muscovite church no longer deferred automatically to the Byzantine Patriarch. Shortly after that, in 1453, Byzantium finally fell to the Ottoman Empire – an event which appalled Moscow's churchmen, but which also vindicated their judgement and liberated them.

By the late 15th century, then, Muscovy was incontestably the dominant power in the north and east of former Kievan Rus, and it had become independent of the Mongols. It had achieved this by integrating most of what had been a dynastic federation into a single patrimony, governed by adapting some Mongol practices.

Its church had emancipated itself from Byzantium and believed it had an ecumenical mission as the bastion of the one true Christian faith. The amalgam of radical centralization with a sense of universal religious calling was to remain the most characteristic feature of Muscovy and later of Russia.

There were at this stage, though, several possible futures before it. It could become an embryonic East Slav nation-state – but the western branches of that potential nation were already under another power. It could become a centre of the eastern Christian ecumene, taking over from Byzantium – but, as we shall see, it was to dilute that mission by assimilating many non-Orthodox, indeed non-Christian, peoples. Or it could become a north Eurasian multi-ethnic and multi-faith empire, in effect the successor to the Golden Horde – but in that case, the church, with its assertive sense of mission and its secular riches, would prove a problematic ally. How these latent conflicts were resolved we shall see in the next chapter.

Chapter 2
The formation of the Muscovite state

In the late 15th and the 16th centuries, the Muscovite state assumed a durable form, which it bequeathed to the Russian Empire. Eurasia was undergoing major upheavals, as the dominant horse-borne steppe overlordships finally yielded to firearms-bearing empires: Ching, Safavid, Mughal, Ottoman, and Muscovite. The Golden Horde had long ago broken up into various smaller khanates, which themselves had little control over raiding Tatar, Nogai, and Kalmyk nomadic bands. By the mid-16th century, the decline of the Hanseatic League and the final eclipse of the Teutonic Knights was creating new opportunities for the nearest powers – Sweden, Denmark, Poland-Lithuania, and Muscovy – but also new dangers, to which all the states responded by far-reaching reforms of governmental control, taxation, and military establishment.

In the Muscovite case, this meant regularly calling up troops to patrol the frontiers or be sent as fast as possible to where they were needed. The Great Prince could do this only by mobilizing the power of junior princes and boyars. Holders of both *votchiny* (hereditary estates) and *pomestia* were required to report regularly for military duty together with their own weapons, horses, and armed men.

The longest and most vulnerable frontier was in the south and east, where nomadic raiders periodically destroyed property and deported local people into slavery. These raiders could be really dangerous: in 1571, Crimean Tatars sacked Moscow itself. To defend its territory, Muscovy began to construct defence lines, consisting of stockades of tree trunks obstructing known raiding routes. Wooden blockhouses and earthen forts were sited at intervals between them. Garrison towns acted as supply depots, bases for the stationing of troops and the despatch of reconnaissance patrols. Initially, the core of the frontier defence forces consisted of light cavalrymen armed with bows, well adapted to steppe warfare. They reported for duty in the spring, summer, or autumn. As military technology advanced, they had to be supplemented by infantry with firearms

Muscovy also enlisted the aid of Cossacks on the Don River – as Poland did those along the lower Dnieper. Cossacks were self-governing military communities who occupied the steppes abandoned by the Golden Horde, hunting, fishing, and occasionally raiding towns or villages on their fringes. Moscow offered them money, arms, and provisions in return for patrolling territory beyond the defence lines. Cossacks, though, were unruly and the arrangement proved at times unreliable.

To coordinate this fighting force over such huge territories required an unprecedented degree of central control. Ivan III and Vasilii III (r. 1505–33) absorbed other Rus princely lands, especially the extensive Novgorod territories, and converted them into *pomestia*. The lesser princes and boyars were given extensive powers to require local communities to fulfil their obligations. The precise terms of military service were laid down by the Service Decree of 1556, which stipulated the weapons, horses, and armed men each *pomeshchik* (estate-holder) had to provide in return for a given quantity of land. *Pomeshchiki* who failed in their duty would lose status and eventually their land as well. A Military Chancery oversaw the implementation of these arrangements: it kept service rosters, ensured that servicemen reported for duty properly equipped, that they were drawn up in formations and directed to their postings, along with all their supplies. This required a complex system of record-keeping – the kernel from which developed the formidable Muscovite/Russian bureaucracy.

The remarkable success of this system eventually gave Muscovy the muscle to conduct offensive operations against the Golden Horde's successor khanates. It conquered Kazan in 1552 and Astrakhan in 1556, thus establishing its ascendancy in the Volga basin and gaining a departure point from which it conquered the Khanate of (Western) Siberia in the late 16th century.

Muscovy also had contested frontiers in the west and north-west, where it launched a campaign in 1558, to gain a direct outlet to the Baltic Sea and prevent any other power dominating the region. The campaign was unsuccessful, since here artillery and trained infantry formations with firearms were vital; Muscovy learned this form of warfare only gradually. Besides, all its fighting there had to be conducted with one eye to the rear, to the danger of raids from the south. This meant its army had to be flexible, disproportionately large for the size of its population, and that good intelligence was crucially important. For this purpose, Muscovy kept envoys posted with all the main Tatar Hordes, collecting information. It was always alert to the possibility of utilizing disagreements within those Hordes and detaching discontented clans to fight on Muscovy's side. This was normal steppe diplomacy.

How did the state raise the resources required for such heavy military commitments? Most of it came in the form of personal service, through the *pomeshchiki* (service estate-holders) reporting with their equipment and retainers. Gradually, taxes came to be levied in a similar way: *pomeshchiki* and the holders of *votchiny* paid the treasury and exacted services from their dependent rural population. Obviously, without reliable peasant input, the service class could not make their contribution to the state's resources, financial and military. The answer was to enserf the peasants. Already by the late 15th century, they were forbidden to quit their lords' estates except around St George's Day (26 November), when harvesting and autumn sowing were complete. During the late 16th and early 17th centuries, when peasant flight increased, this brief loophole was first suspended, then closed altogether. The boundaries of serfdom were finally drawn tight in the Law Code of 1649, which gave the state unlimited powers to track down and reclaim fugitive peasants. Significantly, the Code did not use the words 'serf' or 'serfdom': it merely defined the penalties to be imposed on peasants who fled and on those who harboured them. Nowhere was it stipulated who might become a serf and how he/she might be treated. Serfdom was thus not defined by law but by the evolving practice of personal domination, backed by the state.

Most studies of Russia, rightly, have a lot to say about the central state, yet no less important were local communities. The immense mobilization effort would not have been achieved if they had not been able to deliver. They were organized on the principle of 'joint responsibility' (*krugovaia poruka*). All the inhabitants of a rural or urban settlement were jointly responsible for the payment of taxes, the provision of army recruits, the discharge of labour duties, and the maintenance of peace through the apprehension of troublemakers and criminals. If one household failed in its duties, the other households had to make up the shortfall. Such joint responsibility was common in medieval Europe and Asia, when rulers lacked the administrative apparatus to carry out what we would regard as normal state functions. (In England, the equivalent system was known as 'francpledge'.) The duties of local communities, the service estate, and the laws governing them were set out in the Law Code of 1550.

The ruler who bore the main burden of making this system work was Ivan IV (r. 1533–84 – the 'Terrible'). He aimed to demonstrate beyond doubt that he was undisputed ruler of Rus, that the princes and boyars were his subjects, not partners or even subordinate allies. He insisted on adopting the title of Tsar, the Russian equivalent of Caesar, translatable here as 'sovereign', that is, no longer owing tribute to any earthly ruler. He made some effort to give his authority a broader backing by convening occasional gatherings of representatives of local elites to consult on major issues of policy. Historians have called these gatherings *zemskie sobory* (assemblies of the land), though contemporaries did not use the term. They were not convened regularly, nor was there an established electoral procedure for them. They were occasions, not institutions.

Ivan also intended to establish once and for all that the crown would be hereditary in his family. When in 1553 he fell ill, he required his boyars to take an oath to his son, Dmitry. Many of them were reluctant, and he interpreted their hesitation as treason. He also tended to regard military defeat as evidence of treason among the commanders.

Not altogether without reason. The Lithuanian kingdom, which had competing claims to the lands of Rus, offered its aristocracy higher status and a more effective role in governance. Rus boyars and princes enjoyed a traditional right to choose their own master, and it was always tempting to exercise it and defect to Lithuania. To deter them, Ivan imposed a system of mutual surety on them: if they defected, their extended families or their bail-holders would have to pay large penalties or suffer worse punishment. Failure to give warning of an impending defection was considered an offence, and so the system encouraged denunciations.

In December 1564, Ivan decided to confront 'treason' with an act of theatre. He suddenly withdrew from his court and set out with his family, the state treasury, and several beloved icons for a favourite residence outside Moscow. From there, he sent a missive to the boyars and church leaders accusing them of obstructing his efforts to uncover and root out treason. He demanded the right to proceed against traitors as he saw fit. He also sent a letter to the people of Moscow informing them of his accusations and reassuring them that they had not incurred his wrath. The people sent a petition begging him to return,

> not to leave the country and deliver us to the wolves like unhappy sheep with no shepherd, and to protect us from the strong.... Who will defend us from attack by foreign peoples?... How can we live without a lord?

Here we see one of the recurring themes of Russian history: the ordinary people welcome a strong ruler because he can defend them both from external aggressors and from their own internal strongmen, who exploit them and sometimes fight one another, unleashing destructive warfare in which everyone suffers. When power is mediated through persons rather than institutions, those persons are always liable to give priority to their own individual, family, or factional interests. Ivan, for all his paranoia, was endeavouring to combat this tendency and assert the priority of state service.

His improvised method of doing so was to carve out his own personal territorial realm, in which he would rule as he saw fit. He called it the *oprichnina* – literally, widow's portion. The remaining territory he left to the boyars to rule according to their own customs. In the *oprichnina*, he expropriated most of the boyars and appanage princes, deporting them to the new territories now available around Kazan, and awarded their ancestral lands as *pomestia* to his own servitors. His *oprichniki* rode the country on black horses, each carrying a dog's head and a broom, as it were to sniff out treachery and sweep it away. Supposed traitors were tortured and murdered. Ivan believed that, as God's chosen, uniquely among men he was entitled to commit evil in order to do good. The grotesque cruelty of his campaign, however, divided the elites among themselves and weakened Muscovy's resistance. It was during the *oprichnina* that the Tatars successfully raided Moscow; shortly afterwards, Ivan abolished it.

On the whole, though, boyars accepted the Tsar's dominance, since they recognized that feuding among themselves was mortally dangerous in Muscovy's geopolitically exposed situation. In a sense, the Muscovite polity was the product of a tacit compact between Tsar and boyar elite: the latter acknowledged the Tsar's symbolic omnipotence in return for his ensuring stability and internal peace, including their own dominance over other social orders.

Compared with many of his European contemporaries, Ivan was relatively successful at creating unified authority – though not central control, which was impossible in such a huge and relatively primitive country. This was the impressive side of his achievement. Yet so great were the costs that he left behind him a realm hopelessly overstrained, underpopulated, and devastated. Peasants fled exorbitant taxes and labour dues to seek refuge in monasteries or to try their luck on the open frontier. Above all, he bequeathed a tradition that, to fulfil its demanding functions, the Russian state has to be harsh and domineering, to the extent of violating both human customs and divine laws, and also to depend on personal ties and patron–client networks rather than on stable institutions and laws.

Moreover, Ivan's style of diplomacy impeded the integration of Muscovy into the European diplomatic system. His insistence on the title of Tsar and on precedence over non-hereditary rulers, the failure to develop expertise in European languages and cultures, similar to that which Rus already deployed to deal with the steppe khanates, Byzantium, and the Balkans, all put Muscovy at a disadvantage and closed it to the Renaissance, Reformation, and other developments going forward at the time. In the technical sense, Rus kept up with European military developments, but in other respects remained a closed and rather isolated world of its own.

Orthodox Church

The fall of Byzantium to the Ottoman Turks in 1453 horrified the Christians of Rus. They had been accustomed to look up to the Byzantine church as mentor and patron, ultimate guarantor of their spiritual welfare. Yet at the same time, that disaster opened new opportunities for the Muscovite church. Already wealthy, powerful, and accustomed to speaking for Rus as a whole, it now became the spiritual home of the largest contingent of Orthodox believers in any independent realm. Churchmen began to see Muscovy as successor to Rome and Byzantium, as the 'Third Rome'.

This view was articulated in an epistle of the monk Filofei of Pskov, probably written to Ivan III, warning him against his intention of expropriating ecclesiastical land to award to his military servitors.

> If Thou rulest thine empire rightly, thou wilt be a son of light, and a citizen of the heavenly Jerusalem....And now I say unto thee: take care and take heed....All the empires of Christendom are united....in thine, for two Romes have fallen, the third stands, and there will be no fourth.

The warning was clear: the Muscovite Grand Prince was now responsible for Christendom as a whole. If he failed to rule righteously – for example, if he confiscated church land – the end of the world was at hand: there would be no fourth Rome.

One would have thought this grandiose, if ominous, vision should have appealed to Muscovy's rulers. From their viewpoint, though, it had serious drawbacks. It was issued as a warning *against* expropriating land the Tsar needed for his military servitors. And it implied that the church was the senior partner in their common work, with the right to oversee the Prince's moral conduct. It is significant that only on one occasion shall we find a Muscovite ruler actually citing the concept of 'Moscow the Third Rome'. Yet the idea remained very important to Muscovy's – and later Russia's – Orthodox believers, an ultimate justification for the immense territories and exclusive power claimed by the Princes and Tsars. Russia was to claim the status of champion and protector of the world's true-believing Christians.

It was on this basis that Ivan IV assumed the title of Tsar. The religious outlook underlying his claim was formulated by his leading churchman, Metropolitan Makarii, in a series of texts, excerpts from which were read out in church each Sunday. *The Great Lectionary* and the *Book of Degrees of the Imperial Genealogy*, taken together, resembled the texts compiled in Imperial China to demonstrate that the Emperor had the 'mandate of heaven'. They included sermons, epistles, lives of the saints, and resolutions of church councils, selected and arranged to show that God intended Rus to become His chosen empire on earth. Rus was to be inheritor both of empire and Christian Church: third Rome and second Jerusalem. Each Sunday, believers heard how the Princes of Rus were descended from the Roman Emperor Augustus, and how Vladimir Monomakh had received his regalia from the Byzantine Emperor. This narrative portrayed the Princes of Kiev as intermediaries, and so Muscovy claimed their inheritance too, denying Lithuania's equivalent claims.

When he was crowned Tsar, Ivan IV received from Metropolitan Makarii the Monomakh crown as symbol of the dual derivation of his authority from the universal Christian Church and from the Roman Empire via Byzantium and Kiev. The Patriarch of Constantinople, now subject to the Ottomans, was probably glad to be associated with an external secular ruler: he explicitly acknowledged Ivan's imperial title and addressed him as 'Tsar and Sovereign of Orthodox Christians of the whole Universe [and] among Tsars resembling the apostle-like and ever-glorious Constantine'.

The culmination of this vision of Muscovy came in 1589, when the Metropolitan of Moscow was elevated to the rank of Patriarch. The Ecumenical Patriarch in Constantinople was more ambivalent about this than about Muscovy's imperial claims, since he was here accepting a potential rival. However, he welcomed support and financial aid from Muscovy. Referring to the fate of the previous two Romes, he declared 'Your great Russian empire, the third Rome, has surpassed them all in piety.' Tsar Fedor (r. 1584–98) welcomed this assertion – the only occasion on which a Russian ruler explicitly endorsed the concept of 'Moscow the Third Rome'. In 1589, the synod in Constantinople approved the creation of a fifth Orthodox patriarchate, the first new one created for over a thousand years, and the only one independent of Islamic rule.

This was a development of immense importance. As we shall see, the Orthodox faith was a strong and sufficiently distinctive marker of Russian national identity to survive, and indeed flourish, even in the absence of a Tsar.

17th-century Muscovy

We have seen that Ivan IV almost undid his own achievements through his cruelty and his excessive demands on the people. Furthermore, he undermined the hereditary monarchy he himself had consolidated when in a fit of rage he killed his own heir, leaving only a sickly son, Fedor. Fedor's death in 1598 meant the end of the dynasty and plunged Muscovy into chaos. Onerous service obligations which were (just about) acceptable from a ruler bearing God's blessing proved unacceptable when imposed by a mere boyar, Boris Godunov, even one elected Tsar by a *zemskii sobor*. If nothing else, a boyar monarch inevitably had enemies among other boyars.

And so Muscovy descended into civil war, which has gone down to history as the Time of Troubles. Boyar clans, each with their clients, fought one another. Southern frontier servicemen rebelled against an increasingly demanding state. Cossacks added their own brand of plundering and murdering. In the later stages of the turmoil, both Sweden and Poland became involved, each with its own ambitions to dominate the now fragmented territories and loyalties of Muscovy.

Yet, as it turned out, there was a sufficiently robust sense of identity and potential unity for Muscovy to generate its own revival, especially when faced with the threat of domination by 'heretics'. The decisive factors were Orthodoxy as the national religion, symbolized by the Patriarch, and the resourcefulness of local communities in organizing resistance. When one boyar clan prepared to welcome the Polish royal heir Władisław as constitutional monarch in a personal union with the Polish crown, Patriarch Germogen reacted by insisting that no one should swear loyalty to a Catholic ruler. He sent epistles to elders of the city assemblies, calling on them to mobilize a militia to prevent heretics from taking over Moscow. In Nizhny Novgorod, the merchant Kuzma Minin proclaimed the formation of a militia, and appealed to other cities to do the same:

> Let us be together of one accord...Orthodox Christians in love and unity, and let us not tolerate the recent disorders, but fight untiringly to the death to purge the realm of Muscovy from our enemies, the Poles and Lithuanians.

Detachments came from the various cities to Iaroslavl, on the Volga, under the command of the boyar Prince Dmitry Pozharsky and marched on Moscow, where they expelled the Polish garrison.

The re-establishment of the Muscovite realm was thus mainly the achievement of local communities of joint responsibility, led by boyars, servicemen, urban elites, and Cossacks, and inspired by Muscovy's role as the bastion of Orthodox Christianity. It is understandable, then, that the *zemskii sobor* which was summoned by the Patriarch in 1613 rejected all foreign candidates to the throne and restored the political model inherited from Ivan IV. Its delegates elected as Tsar Mikhail Romanov (r. 1613–45), descendant of the family of Ivan's first wife. They imposed no conditions on him: the overriding priority was to restore a stable Muscovite realm with a strong ruler. It was expected, though, that he would consult with his elites before taking major decisions.

Seventeenth-century Muscovy was, then, ruled along the same lines as in the 16th. The royal family, the court, and the administrative chanceries grew in size, but did not change their essential nature: they supplied vital central coordination to the mobilization of people and resources taking place in the localities. Assemblies, such as the Boyar Duma and the *zemskii sobor*, which connected the centre with those localities, remained weakly developed and uninstitutionalized, though at times they played a crucial role in the formation of policy. What was permanent were the boyar and service noble clans, with their clientele networks in towns and villages throughout the country.

The link with the localities was reinforced by military governors (*voevody*) appointed by the Tsar. They increasingly operated according to codified law and written instructions, and they were required to make frequent reports on local conditions. However, the *voevody* lacked specialized legal training, and they depended for part of their income on *kormlenie*, so that much of what they achieved they owed to personal links with their subordinates. To prevent those links becoming too cosy, they were normally appointed for only two years at a time. All the same, these personalized central–local ties were to remain characteristic of Russian governance.

During the 17th century, the chanceries developed into an effective and differentiated early modern bureaucracy, dealing in ever greater detail not only with military matters, but with finance, post, and communications, the assignment of service lands, and relations with other states. An elite lineage hierarchy (*mestnichestvo*) determined entry into the chanceries, but thereafter promotion depended on merit. Officials were bound by oaths of loyalty and secrecy, which became an integral part of Russian state culture. That culture ensured that high officials, though often corrupt and self-enriching, did not engage in oppositional politics. The very success of these governing bodies in coping with the crises of the 17th century increased their relative power and inhibited the formation of intermediate bodies which might have mediated their relationship with the population. The only competing institution was the church, which still had its charters and wealth inherited from the past.

Meanwhile, warfare was posing ever-changing technical and human demands. The extension of Muscovite territory was drawing in new peoples, with their own cultures, religions, and polities: Muscovy was becoming Russia. This process required adjustments which were sometimes destabilizing. In 1648, the Dnieper Cossacks rebelled against the Polish crown and appealed to the Tsar to come to their aid. Their Hetman (leader) promised him 'eternal loyalty' in return for receiving supplies and the confirmation of their privileges. With their aid, Muscovy occupied Kiev and the whole of eastern Ukraine. This was a great triumph, but one achieved on the basis of a misunderstanding. The Cossacks considered their promise conditional on Muscovy continuing to fulfil its side of the agreement. The Tsar, however, regarded them as a service nobility which had pledged him eternal loyalty and subjection. During the following decades, Ukraine gradually became an integral part of the empire, yet one whose elites never wholly lost their yearning for greater freedom.

In preparing for war, Muscovy had both weaknesses and strengths. It had to borrow the latest military techniques from abroad, hence often imported foreign officers and mercenaries. Muscovy's authority structure was relatively simple, however: it had few of the privileged intermediary institutions which obstructed military–fiscal reform in many European countries. As a result, once military innovations had been absorbed, they could be disseminated and corresponding service obligations enforced with a minimum of friction. The accompanying cultural transformation took much longer, though.

Territorial expansion likewise entailed advantages and disadvantages. On the one hand, Russia's relatively simple personalized political structure often made it easy to incorporate a new ethos: its elites became part of the empire's branch network, and continued often to exercise their power in much the same way as previously. On the other hand, sometimes Russia's economy and culture was at a more primitive level than those of newly absorbed peoples, who therefore chafed at Russia's dominance. More fundamentally, Russia's Orthodox identity faced challenges coping with the new, sometimes hostile, religions being incorporated in the empire.

The church schism

The first crisis which posed such challenges was the schism of the mid-17th century. Many viewed the Time of Troubles as God's punishment for the church's sins, and so a movement had grown up to correct and coordinate the conduct of the liturgy and to purify the morals of clergy and believers. Like their counterparts in several European countries, both Catholic and Protestant, they aimed to tidy up church services and to purge religious life of folk practices. The Zealots of Piety, as they were known, objected to drinking, dancing, bear-baiting, and to the profane and sometimes obscene performances of the strolling players (*skomorokhi*). They became influential at the court of Tsar Aleksei (r. 1645–76), and one of their number, Metropolitan Nikon of Novgorod, was elected Patriarch in 1652.

Nikon's reforming motives differed, however, from those of his colleagues. Whereas they were concerned entirely with the

Muscovite church, he had a broader agenda. Encouraged by the recent annexation of the Ukrainian Hetmanate, he aimed to turn the Moscow Patriarchate into an ecumenical patriarchate, an Eastern Rome, dominant over both the Tsar and the other Orthodox churches. To render the Muscovite church worthy of its grandiose mission, however, he wanted to be sure that its practices accorded with the rites of the ancient ecumenical church. His contact with Greek and Ukrainian churchmen had alerted him to discrepancies between their texts and rituals and those of Muscovy. Assuming that the Muscovite versions were recent errors, he assembled variant texts and scholars, including some from Greece, Ukraine, and even Italy, to make corrections.

As a result of their studies, he ordered a slight amendment in the spelling of 'Jesus' and instructed congregations to make a number of liturgical changes, including reciting three Alleluias after the Psalms instead of two and making the sign of the cross with three fingers instead of two. None of these changes had any doctrinal significance, but for largely illiterate congregations, every detail of the liturgy was sacrosanct. Moreover, Nikon violated custom by imposing the changes without convening a church council to endorse them.

Tsar Aleksei supported him. His motives, however, were different, imperial rather than ecumenical. He wanted the church's practices reformed so that it could support the state in spreading its authority in the empire's new lands. He required a supportive church, not a dominant one. Besides, he increasingly found Nikon's supercilious behaviour repugnant and gradually cooled towards him. In 1658, offended by Aleksei's aloofness, Nikon dramatically doffed his patriarchal robes in the middle of divine service and put on the simple habit of a monk. Aleksei accepted his resignation, but continued to support his reforms. Anxious to obtain endorsement from Constantinople, he invited Greek prelates to the church council of 1666–7. They were delighted to enforce Greek norms and invalidate the practices of the Russian church since it had broken with Constantinople in the 15th century. The council not only confirmed the reforms but pronounced anathema on those who rejected them as heretics and schismatics.

Opposition to the reforms came from those who objected to what seemed to them alien violations of long-consecrated Russian practice. 'If we are schismatics,' they argued, 'then the holy fathers, Tsars and Patriarchs were also schismatics.' Their protestations resonated with all those who opposed the church's increasing institutionalization, the imposition from above of stereotyped liturgical forms, and the extirpation of 'pagan' practices. The Old Belief, as this opposition came to be called, thus had widespread support from both elites and masses. It provided a rallying point for all who objected to a more impersonal, centralized, and bureaucratic style of government, to Polonized Baroque architecture, or to the adoption of Western clothing and the import of Western books.

It is difficult to exaggerate the importance of the Old Belief. It has survived to the present day, and indeed at times flourished, in spite of intermittent official persecution. It retained the vision which had enabled Muscovy to survive the Tatar overlordship, expand, and then come through the Time of Troubles – a vision of a world of local communities united by personal reverence of the Tsar, by the one true faith, and by obedience to *pravda*. Old Believers rejected a Latinate faith enforced by official decree and subservient priests. They became bearers of the old Muscovite messianic national myth in opposition to the new Russian imperial state, which the more radical among them regarded as the work of the Antichrist. The idea of Russia as the 'Third Rome', the 'new Israel', with its own 'chosen people', remained as an evocative substratum in Russian culture, always ready to re-emerge in one form or another.

4. Old Believers in Nizhny Novgorod

In the 18th century, Peter I and Catherine II took the work of Aleksei to its logical conclusion in subordinating the church to the state. Peter abolished the Patriarchate, replacing it with a Holy Synod, a council of leading bishops which could be and sometimes was chaired by a layman. Catherine expropriated church lands and replaced the income from them with a stipend amounting to only about a quarter of its value. Meanwhile, the top–down 'regularization' of church life continued, mediated by priests appointed by bishops rather than elected by parishes. Priests became a segregated social estate, marked out from the rest of secularized and Westernized elite society by a separate education system and by non-Western dress.

Popular discontent

Of the feelings of ordinary people about this system of government and about serfdom, its consequence, we have little direct evidence. We have to judge from their actions and from the documents of officials and military men who were usually alien to them and sometimes their opponents. Serfdom and joint responsibility did offer peasants some advantages. It guaranteed them land – something of which English rural dwellers at the same period could not be confident – a community for mutual support, not unconditional but usually available, and a parish church for spiritual sustenance. They had their own self-governing assemblies, and on the whole they determined their own agrarian practices, or at least fashioned them by negotiation with the landowner's steward.

Yet serfdom constrained their freedom of movement, imposed taxes and/or heavy labour obligations on them, and at times military service. It usually provided subsistence, but on meagre soils in a harsh climate where cultivation was marginal and might be threatened by bad weather or by extra demands from superiors. Their relationship with their landlord, if they had one, was ambivalent: he could be a source of patronage and protection, but on the other hand, his demands were unpredictable, not effectively restrained by anyone, and sometimes ruinously onerous. At all times, there were peasants who found these conditions intolerable and left the village illegally to seek a better life in the more fertile south, or in the Urals and Siberia where there was plentiful land and no landlords. Refugees from the system, those mobile peasants paradoxically often became its agents in extending assimilated territory far to the south and east.

The 17th and 18th centuries were a time of especially pronounced popular discontent among peasants, townsfolk, Cossacks, and steppe tribes. As we have seen above, the state was not only imposing increasing burdens, it was becoming more bureaucratic. What caused the discontent was not so much the burdens themselves as the violation of traditional moral norms, of legitimate hierarchy and authority, held by communities to be both time-honoured and in accordance with *pravda*. Most rebellions came from the less settled south and east, and originated in local communities whose obligations had abruptly changed. They usually began not with peasants, but with Cossacks or recently annexed non-Russian peoples, as in the Razin rebellion of 1667–71 and the Pugachev rebellion of 1773–5. Many Cossacks objected vehemently to the Tsar's attempts to register them, make them subjects, and incorporate them fully into his army. Bashkir, Kalmyk, and Nogai tribesmen resented the erosion of their traditional freedoms. Russians had similar grievances, though: restless peasants would join the non-Russians and avenge their own grievances by attacking *pomeshchik* estates, plundering, burning, and murdering as they went.

The Pugachev rebellion (1773–5) fed on just such grievances. The Yaik Cossacks of the southern Urals had traditionally been able to elect their own leaders (atamans), and had considerable freedom of action provided they patrolled and defended the frontier lines around Orenburg, where the integration of the Kazakh steppe was beginning. During the 1750s, the Tsar abolished those freedoms and integrated them into the regular Russian army. The Cossacks rose under Emelian Pugachev, who had converted to the Old Belief and assumed the title of the recently deposed Tsar Peter III (see below, p. 42). His manifesto was an exemplary statement of popular grievances and projected a vision of a fair and righteous hierarchy of authority. It accused the *pomeshchiki* of having violated 'the ancient tradition of the Christian law' and supplanted it with 'an alien law taken from German traditions'. He promised that

> By God's grace, We, Peter III, Emperor and Autocrat of all the
> Russias.... with royal and fatherly charity grant by this our
> personal ukaz to all who were previously peasants and subjects of
> the *pomeshchiki* to be true and loyal servants of our throne, and
> we reward them with the ancient cross and prayer [Old Belief],
> with bearded heads, with liberty and freedom and to be for ever
> Cossacks, demanding neither recruit enlistment, poll tax nor other

money dues....And we free peasants and all the people from the taxes and burdens which were previously imposed by wicked nobles and mercenary urban judges.

Pugachev was soon joined by downgraded Tatar nobles, Bashkirs whose grazing lands had been expropriated, and serfs assigned to Urals factories. Enserfed peasants, encouraged by their marauding, and indignant that nobles had recently been emancipated from state service while the peasants had not, attacked *pomeshchik* estates, and in some cases murdered their owners. Once again, a great fear stalked Russia, until Empress Catherine II could send an army, which eventually restored order.

In the 19th century, there were no mass risings on this scale, but low-level discontent continued to simmer, finding an outlet in sporadic acts of peasant resistance, as multiple volumes of documents published by Soviet scholars demonstrate. The durable symbiosis of government, *pomeshchiki*, and peasant communities continued to offer some benefits to both sides, but also generated resentment and conflict, which impeded the assimilation of the majority of the people into the political community and left a permanent latent threat of disorder.

Chapter 3
The Russian Empire and Europe

State and society

It fell to Peter the Great (r. 1682–1725) to take aboard the full implications of Russia becoming an empire and European great power. He did not change the fundamental structure of Russian society, indeed he consolidated it. But he transformed the symbolism of authority and the culture of the elites. He adopted the Latin title *Russorum Imperator*. He implicitly repudiated the Orthodox justification of autocracy by abandoning the annual Palm Sunday ritual of riding on a donkey led by the Patriarch. He believed he did not need the church's guidance, but was directly answerable to God for the greatness and security of his state and for the welfare of his people.

He was convinced that these aims could be achieved only by making Russia a fully European country. His eulogists boasted of his having dragged Russia 'from darkness into light'. Early in his reign, he visited the Netherlands and England, worked as an apprentice in their shipyards, and became fascinated with the latest technology, especially in the naval and military field. Returning to Russia, he issued a constant stream of laws and edicts. After mixed military fortunes during the early years of his reign, he created Russia's first standing army, manned by soldiers who served for life. It was financed by a poll tax, a source of revenue easy to compute and to collect through the landlords, who could enforce joint responsibility for payment on their subordinate villages. The soldiers were ordinary peasants chosen by their landlord or by the village assembly.

When peasants joined the army, their lives were transformed. They left the village in effect for ever – and some village societies would actually arrange a symbolic funeral for them. They ceased to be serfs and gained a few modest rights – a uniform, regular pay, and the chance of promotion or decoration. They became in a sense the first demotic imperial citizens. Their lives, of course, were exceedingly gruelling, especially given the harsh nature of military discipline, but all the same their morale and *esprit de corps* were on the whole good, and they fought with enthusiasm and determination. Foreigners began to conceive a greater respect for the Russian army. Peter's reform initiated a period of military success. In 1709, at the Battle of Poltava, Russia decisively defeated Sweden, its greatest rival in northern Europe, and went on to conquer its Baltic provinces. Russia was ahead of other European powers in creating a national army, and as long as successful conscription and supply remained the principal conditions for success, that army thrived.

Scarcely less important, Peter created a navy and stationed it on the Baltic, declaring thereby Russia's intention of establishing a permanent presence in Europe's seas. Having conquered territory in Ingria, at the eastern extremity of the Gulf of Finland, he began construction of a new city there, St Petersburg. Soon, its shipyards were teeming with workers constructing the frames of a new battle fleet, whose headquarters were at Kronstadt, on an island a few miles down the Gulf.

St Petersburg was much more than a naval base: it soon became the new capital of the empire, created to mark Peter's

5. An equestrian portrait of Peter the Great

determination to break into the European constellation of powers. Its design showed that he also intended to adopt European architectural styles and European patterns of political and social life. Architects from several European countries designed its public buildings. Its main thoroughfares radiated out from the Admiralty building on the River Neva; senior noble families constructed their palaces in the latest Baroque style on those avenues and along the canals which intersected them, on the model of Amsterdam. In their spacious staterooms, Peter ordered that salons, balls, and

39

other social gatherings be held, in which women, hitherto barred from grand social occasions, were required to participate. He wanted Russian nobles to take their rightful place in the European diplomatic world, where such socializing was *de rigueur*. Nobles and merchants were required to abandon Muscovite kaftans and don Western-style jackets, waistcoats, and breeches. They were ordered to cut off their beards, a compulsion which many found offensive, even sacrilegious, since for Orthodox believers a beard was a sign of masculine dignity bestowed by God. Those who resisted shaving had to submit to the humiliation of having it done forcibly and publicly.

Peter also endeavoured to create what he called a 'regular state', adopting European patterns of government, with Sweden and England as his preferred models. He replaced the old chanceries with 'colleges', whose collective administrative boards were meant to ensure that merit rather than patronage determined appointments.

Peter wanted to ensure that government was conducted by responsible and qualified officials. Nobles were required to acquire training in a skill useful to the state, whether civilian or military; their promotion was to depend on their proven merit and experience. His Table of Ranks for military, civilian, and court service stipulated the requirements for each rung of the hierarchy. Army officers even had to go through a period as private soldiers to gain the right to a commission. Nobles were at first aghast at these impositions, but they soon discovered that they were in a far better position to acquire and benefit from education than any other social estate. Meritocracy modified but did not endanger their domination of the political system and social life.

Among Peter's most fateful measures was his reform of the Orthodox Church. He abolished the Patriarchate, which, as we have seen, was intended to give the Russian church superior status in the Orthodox ecumene, and replaced it with an administrative board known as the Holy Synod, which consisted mainly of senior bishops, but whose chairman could be and sometimes was a layman, appointed by the Emperor. Feofan Prokopovich, his Jesuit-trained ecclesiastical adviser, argued that the Byzantine 'symphony' of Tsar and Patriarch had misled believers into imagining that Russia had two equal rulers. He advanced the Hobbesian view that human beings were by nature avaricious and belligerent; without a single unambiguous sovereign, there would be endless civil war. This implied that the ruler's will was not limited by God's law, since it was itself an expression of God's law. Peter certainly believed that.

In many respects, the church now became a constituent component of the state. Monasteries were required to function as agents of social security, offering help to the poor, the sick, and army veterans. Parish priests were trained to offer consistent and correct liturgical forms; they were increasingly appointed from above on meritocratic principles, rather than elected by parish councils. They were, moreover, instructed to report anything potentially endangering state security which they might hear in the confessional: their political duty was to override their pastoral obligations.

Peter's church reform was in some respects Protestant in form, inspired by the examples of Sweden, Holland, and England. Yet the Russian church lacked many of the features that underpinned Protestantism in those countries: a literate population, scriptures in the vernacular, and active parish councils. Essentially, Peter continued the work of Aleksei, remoulding the church to make it useful to empire. He thereby deepened the split between the church and the old national myth. To many Old Believers, Peter was the Antichrist, abjuring the good old Russian ways in favour of heretical 'German' abominations.

There was an ineluctable paradox at the heart of Peter's intended transformation of Russia: he wanted to inspire Russians to initiative and achievement, but by command from above. He abolished collective petitions and repeatedly interfered where he felt initiative from below was inadequate or misdirected. His personal agents, *fiskaly*, kept a constant eye on officials and reported on their transgressions. For all the symbolic innovations, in most respects he consolidated the fundamental structure of Russian society as he had inherited it from Muscovy. He did nothing to fill the gap between the monarchy and local communities; on the contrary, he intensified the hierarchical and personal nature of such links as existed.

His project had the support of most of the elites, not least because it was successful in military terms. As a result, though Russia had relatively weak rulers after Peter, it was not threatened by the breakdown of authority, and continued to enhance its status among European powers. Top nobles and senior army officers were prepared to work together with the monarch to maintain social stability and military preparedness. As in Muscovy, they had a shared interest in doing so, to forestall internal unrest and prevent external invasion. That tacit agreement was formulated in each accession manifesto, which stated that the monarch was elected and approved by the people: in practice, this meant that he/she was accepted by the most influential nobles and army officers, with the Guards usually playing a decisive role. Monarchs who were not acceptable in this sense were swiftly deposed, as happened in 1762 to Peter III (r. 1761–2), who managed to alienate those very circles.

The underlying rationale of this synergy between monarchy and nobility was illuminated in 1730, when Peter II (r. 1727–30), grandson of Peter I, suddenly died. With no male heir in view, a privy council dominated by two very well-connected families, the Golitsyns and Dolgorukys, decided to offer the throne to Anna, daughter of Ivan V (see the Chronology), under conditions which would have limited her power and inaugurated an oligarchic regime like that of contemporary Sweden or Britain.

Nobles of lesser rank also managed to present proposals to Anna. These likewise envisaged the monarch consulting noble representatives in some kind of assembly, but imposed no express limitations on her. This was close to the traditional Muscovite conception of monarchy, though articulated in language which reflected contemporary European experience of constitutionalism. Anna accepted the alternative proposals and dramatically tore up the privy council document in public. In this way, she perpetuated the tradition of autocratic rule by agreement with broader elites rather than with an exclusive clique of magnates. She demonstrated her devotion to nobles' interests by establishing a Cadet Corps exclusively for them: they could be trained there and advance directly to officer status rather than endure a humiliating apprenticeship as private soldiers.

The monarch's power was still *de facto* limited, no longer by God's law, but by a nobility which manipulated patronage and kinship in its own interests, but also cared deeply about the security and prosperity of Russia. They were the principal stakeholders in the empire.

This mutual compact left the nobles free to impose their own arrangements on those subject to them, their serfs, and on the lower orders generally. Historians used to believe that serfdom was scarcely distinguishable from slavery. It is true that *pomeshchiki* exercised virtually total control over their serfs, including even buying and selling them. Recent research has, however, suggested that Russian peasant society was a good deal more resilient and self-reliant than the term 'slavery' implies. Serfdom at least gave most peasants entitlement to land – a benefit denied to US plantation slaves.

Living in a harsh climate and on relatively infertile soils, most Russian peasants strove above all to limit risk, and at this they were remarkably successful. Subsistence crises were relatively rare, though when they struck they were extremely serious.

The strip system of land tenure guaranteed each household arable land of different qualities, while pastures and meadows were held in common. The periodic redistribution of strips ensured that each household had enough resources to feed itself and make its contribution to the village's dues and obligations. Joint responsibility ensured that peasants had to take decisions in common and had an interest in helping each other through difficulties. They also kept a sharp eye on each other's behaviour, since the failure of any one household imposed burdens on all the others. If a household was failing chronically, its neighbours could be ruthless in trying to expel it from the village. Wastrels, weaklings, and drunkards were not tolerated indefinitely.

This agrarian system was successful at providing Russia with resources (army recruits, taxes, and other obligations), ensuring the survival and even growth of the rural population, and underwriting the well-being of the nobility. It was the backbone of the empire.

Russia and Europe

Russia was becoming a European power at a time when Europe itself was changing. The Peace of Westphalia (1648) had ended the period when one single power could hope to dominate the continent, and Europe had become a cluster of sovereign states jostling among themselves for power and influence. That process required the gradual codification of international law and the stationing of permanent envoys in each other's territories to maintain communications. Each state needed to constantly renew its military technology, and to mobilize its natural resources to the maximum, which in turn entailed investing in science and technology. Having robust armed forces and a productive economy required concern for the well-being, education, and training of the population. Statesmen were beginning to concern themselves with the 'public welfare' even of their humbler subjects; thinkers were becoming more concerned with the citizen's input into the political process, the rule of law, and limitations on the ruler's power.

This was the constellation of great powers which Russia joined in the 18th century. The response of European countries was ambivalent. From the early 18th century, and especially after the Seven Years War (1756–63), no one could deny that Russia was a member of the European 'club': its military victories spoke for themselves. All the same, Europe's elites still regarded Russia as being in some way alien: its sheer size and massive population, its immense resources, its military might, its semi-Asiatic geography, its ever-expanding frontiers, and its uncertain ambitions all inclined European statesmen to regard it with suspicion and distrust.

Russia really had no choice but to make itself amenable to this disdainful 'club'. To defend its long and mostly open frontiers, to deal with threats of sedition among its very diverse populations, Russia needed not only a powerful army and navy, but also friendly relations with its European neighbours, sometimes achieved by royal marriages. It also needed where possible to gain confidential knowledge of European powers' intentions and capabilities.

For that reason, from Peter I onwards, Russia's statesmen gave priority to training noblemen in European languages and sending them on tours around the European capitals to participate in polite society and to get to know the intentions of the courts and the peoples' customs. The new Cadet Corps which trained future army officers in ballistics and fortification also taught them music, dancing, social etiquette, and foreign languages. Graduates spoke excellent French and were soon to be found mixing gracefully with high society in France and Germany. Moreover, Catherine II herself as Empress corresponded with Voltaire and Diderot, two leading thinkers of the European Enlightenment.

The inevitable result was to create a yawning gap between the way of life of the ordinary people and that of Russia's elites, who gradually became more numerous during the 18th and 19th centuries. This gap was especially damaging to the church, whose culture changed far less than that of secular elites.

The effort seemed to pay off, though. In the 18th century, Russia had remarkable military and diplomatic successes. The greatest geostrategic obstacle to its great power position was its land-locked location. Despite its immense size, it could conduct sea trade with Europe only through the Gulf of Finland or the White Sea, both of which could become iced over in winter. Having gained the former Baltic provinces of Sweden, Russia dismembered the Polish-Lithuanian Commonwealth and annexed its capital, Warsaw, through diplomatic agreements with Austria and Prussia.

The Ottoman Empire still dominated the Black Sea, which became Russia's prime target during the 18th and early 19th centuries. Russia gained a series of victories over the Ottomans, annexed the Crimea (the first Ottoman Muslim territory to fall under Christian control), colonized fertile lands on the Black Sea coast, and established the major port of Odessa to carry the new international trade through the Bosphorus. Its army was, however, unable to advance as far as Constantinople because of geographical obstacles: the swampy Danube delta, rivers, and mountains. The alternative route to Turkey through the Caucasus was rendered hazardous by the mountain peoples, most of whom were Muslim or converted to Islam in the course of facing Russian aggression. Moreover, Russia knew that any final offensive directed at Constantinople would risk dragging other European powers into a general war which would overstrain Russia's resources.

'Regularizing' the state

Catherine II (the Great, r. 1762–96) attempted to broaden the social and cultural basis of the monarchy and to give it a foundation of legality, as that was understood in 18th-century Europe. She herself came to the throne through a Guards coup against her husband, Peter III, and so needed extra legitimation. This is not the only explanation of her concern for institutions, however. She was an eager student of European Enlightenment political thinkers, and in 1767 she undertook an unusually bold experiment to establish a 'legal monarchy': she convened an elected Legislative Commission to create a new Law Code. This was not just a return to the Muscovite practice of occasional consultation with elites: Catherine's Commission was broadly elected and represented state officials, nobles, merchants, Cossacks, state peasants, and non-Russian communities; the only absentees were serfs and clergymen. As in France two decades later, deputies brought with them from their electors petitions and proposals for reform. Catherine never intended the Commission to limit her power; as she stated in the lengthy document she put before it, she believed in absolute rule since 'there is no other authority...that can act with a vigour proportionate to the extent of such a vast domain'. But she did want it to establish law as a basis for that absolute rule.

In the event, she was disappointed. The proposals of the various estates displayed a predominant concern with their own narrowly conceived interests, rather than with the needs of the state or the population as a whole. It was difficult to fashion a new Law Code out of them, and at the outbreak of the Turkish war in 1768 Catherine prorogued the sessions. She never reconvened the Commission, but did use its materials in further lawmaking. She correctly discerned that Russia's greatest need was for 'intermediate' institutions between the state and the population. She tried to provide for them by creating new local government institutions, provinces (*gubernii*) and districts (*uezdy*), in which the nobility would play the main role. Peter III had already freed the nobility from the obligation to perform state service. She went further: her Charter to the Nobility (1785) guaranteed its property, freed it from corporal punishment, and allowed it to set up its own

6. A contemporary portrait of Catherine the Great

assemblies in each *guberniia* and *uezd*, with power to appoint
local officials.

She issued a parallel charter to the cities. Together, they fixed the
form of local government and much of provincial social and
political life until the 1917 revolution. The nobles became the only
estate to have guaranteed rights, and this fact meant that serfdom
became even more arbitrary: serfs had no legal protection against

abuse. Russia was now run by a ruling class with its own defined rights, with a Europeanized culture and complete power over the persons of its serfs. This internal cultural and social gulf defined Russian life for the next century. The serfs, for their part, were perfectly capable of discerning that, while they still had state obligations, their superiors had none.

The brief reign of Emperor Paul (r. 1796–1801) illustrated what happened when an Emperor broke the convention that he should rule with the consent of the elite. Paul took the view, which would have been applauded by most peasants, that the nobles' privileges were unjustified. He abolished their exemption from state service, closed down their provincial associations, and instead appointed local officials himself. He decreed that their estates should be taxed on the same basis as peasant land. He ended their freedom from corporal punishment, and curtailed their right to travel abroad and to receive foreign literature. At the same time, he gave peasants the right to petition him personally about mistreatment at the hands of their lords.

There is little doubt that Paul's personality was unbalanced. He was given to sudden changes of mood and uncontrollable attacks of rage, when he would insult even his highest officials and advisers. The same, though, had been true of Peter the Great. In 1801, however, a group of Guards officers, led by the governor-general of St Petersburg, deposed Paul, with the consent of his son, Alexander. They then went on to murder him – something to which Alexander had not consented. Paul's innovations were then quietly retracted.

Alexander (r. 1801–25) was well aware of the injustices Paul had tried in his clumsy way to rectify, but he took a very different approach to them. Up to the end of the 18th century, Russia's leaders assumed that Russia would create for itself a 'regular' state similar to those evolving in the other European powers. Alexander I began his reign in this spirit, elaborating proposals to consolidate the rule of law and introduce representative institutions. But he faced an intractable dilemma. He could proceed by enhancing the freedoms of the nobility: but that would imply augmenting their privileges and intensifying social inequality. Or he could try to extend civil rights more broadly to the population as a whole: but that could be accomplished only by overriding the nobles and thus strengthening autocracy. In the course of his reign, he made serious plans in both directions, but brought neither to fulfilment.

In the end, Alexander's most durable reform was the creation of functional ministries, each headed by a single minister who took responsibility for its work. This novelty, derived from European models, did something to introduce order and system into government. However, since there were no regular cabinet meetings and no prime minister, the task of coordinating government fell as before on the Emperor, consulting with individual ministers; this arrangement thus retained personal relationships at the heart of government. Moreover, the Ministry of the Interior was responsible for policing the entire empire and for overseeing all provincial institutions; it was thus much larger than any other, and its priorities tended to overshadow other governmental functions.

The war against Napoleon

Russia's vulnerability, but also the geopolitical resources at its disposal, were dramatically illustrated by the war against Napoleon in 1812. When it invaded, the Grande Armée was larger and more experienced than the Russian army. The only way to deny it victory was to retreat indefinitely, avoiding major battles and making use of Russia's spaces and (eventually) severe climate to wear it down. Russia could mobilize men and resources from a rich and diverse reserve of food, raw materials, equipment, and manpower – though only slowly because of the distances. Yet endless retreat entailed terrible suffering, the destruction of homes, equipment, animals, and crops, the demoralization of both the civilian and military population. No one dared to announce this strategy openly, since it implied such horrific sacrifices. On the contrary, Alexander and his commander, Barclay de Tolly, originally declared their intention to retreat only a certain distance, to fortified lines where they hoped they could make a stand. Each time the Russian army reached such a line, however, Napoleon proved too threatening, and after skirmishes it resumed its retreat.

Eventually, Alexander decided the army had to make a stand before Moscow, and to implement his decision appointed a commander with an impeccably Russian surname, Mikhail Kutuzov, hero of Catherine's wars. The result was the huge Battle of Borodino, technically a Russian defeat, after which the Grande Armée resumed its advance, but in a weakened condition. Kutuzov decided that his forces could no longer defend Moscow and therefore abandoned the city – which was soon consumed by fire. Napoleon was appalled at the spectacle: 'This is a war of extermination', he exclaimed, 'a terrible strategy which has no precedents in the history of civilisation! ... What ferocious determination! What a people!' He still assumed he would soon receive envoys from the Tsar, suing for peace. But no one came to treat with him, and eventually he decided it was impossible to spend the winter in a devastated city.

On the miserable and seemingly endless march westwards out of Russia, the dwindling Grande Armée was constantly harassed by guerrilla forces, small detachments which would suddenly emerge from the forest, kill stragglers and seize supplies, then vanish again. They consisted of peasants, though always under the command of regular officers. Alexander was nervous of mobilizing peasant volunteers, since he rightly assumed they would want to be freed from serfdom as a reward for doing their civic duty. Indeed, there were some disturbances where peasants tried to volunteer and resisted being turned away by recruiting sergeants.

7. A woodcut of Napoleon's winter retreat from Moscow

Europe as a source of ideas

The Napoleonic War illustrated what the Russian state could gain from its European links. Russian diplomats had used to good effect their contacts among the Parisian elite, some of whom were indiscreet and not well disposed to Napoleon. As a result, Alexander knew well in advance when Napoleon was intending to attack Russia in 1812 and how he planned to do so. Without that knowledge, Russia might well have lost the war.

Yet those contacts also held dangers for Russia's internal stability. Its Europeanized elites brought back home with them French and German ideas: in turn, Pietism, Enlightenment legalism and secularism, Freemasonry, Romanticism, Hegelian idealism, and eventually socialism. Russia offered the first example of what later became known as a 'developing country', whose elites were attracted by European culture, yet also resented it as a disruption of a traditional way of life. Broadly speaking, they were divided into two camps: 'Westerners' took it for granted that Russia was moving in the same direction as what they called 'the West', if rather more slowly, while 'Slavophiles' denied this and took a pride in Russia's distinctiveness.

In the former camp, many felt that victory over France rendered even more intolerable the absence of citizenship or the rule of law. When Alexander died suddenly in December 1825, a group of army officers imbued with such ideals tried to stage a coup in St Petersburg. The rebellion of the Decembrists (as they became known) was improvised and was easily put down, but it left Alexander's successor, Nicholas I (r. 1825–55), feeling threatened and anxious, determined to make no concessions to liberal sentiment.

Others argued that victory proved Russia was not just a backward European country: its distinctive institutions had their own virtues. Nikolai Karamzin, Russia's first modern historian, for example, asserted that Russia's autocracy was not its shame but its glory; indeed, it had played the vital formative role without which Russia would not even exist as a state. Even the poet Alexander Pushkin, who had felt some sympathy with the Decembrists, argued that Russia was justified in suppressing the Polish rebellion of 1830. His acquiescence in this imperial coercion is especially striking since he was not an unreserved admirer of the form the empire had taken. In his poem *The Bronze Horseman*, he extols St Petersburg as a great and beautiful capital city. Yet he also bemoans the fate of one of its humble inhabitants, who has lost his beloved in one of the floods to which it was susceptible as a result of being built in an unsuitable marshy location. Evgenii shakes his fist impotently at a horse-borne statue of Peter the Great, then flees in terror, imagining he hears the horseman pursuing him through the streets. Later he is found, dead.

Nicholas I's education minister, Count Uvarov, articulated Karamzin's view in what became a semi-official catchphrase: Orthodoxy, Autocracy, Nationality. It implied that Russia owed its greatness to its own church, the untrammelled authority of its monarch, and the patriotic devotion of its people, whose effectiveness had been proved in 1812.

Nicholas himself accepted this view wholeheartedly. He resisted calls for an end to serfdom, even though he called it 'an obvious and palpable evil', since abolishing it would destabilize the empire. He turned his face against a constitution for the same reason and governed in authoritarian style with the aid of officers who had distinguished themselves in the Napoleonic campaign. He did, though, see the importance of consistent laws, even if, like his police chief, Benkendorf, he considered that 'Laws are written for subjects, not for governments'. He promoted the promulgation of a new Digest of Laws, and created an Imperial School of Jurisprudence, where a later generation of senior officials received a serious training in law as an autonomous branch of science.

An especially radical challenge to Uvarov's homespun pride was offered by a letter circulating in the salons in the early 1830s, written by a Guards officer, Petr Chaadaev. He asserted that Russia did not belong to the European Christian family of nations, but neither was it a properly Asiatic country. Suspended in between, it was a kind of black hole in civilization:

> Alone in the world, we have given nothing to the world, learned nothing from the world, and bestowed not a single idea upon the fund of human ideas.

The Slavophiles affirmed that, on the contrary, Russia did have its own distinct and valuable contribution to make. It had preserved the integrity of Orthodox Christianity, which in most of Europe had been destroyed either by power-loving Popes or by rationalist, individualist Protestants. The spirit of community (*sobornost*), which the church had upheld, was also exemplified in the peasant community and the workmen's cooperative (*artel*), where resources were shared and periodically redistributed to reflect the changing needs of individual households. In the West, human beings were spiritually impoverished, tainted by a mercenary *laissez-faire* economy, by individualism, rationalism, and atheism. Russia's *sobornost* would heal the West's ailments. In this way, the Slavophiles made a virtue of Russia's local communities of joint responsibility. But they also warned that Russia's monarchy was itself, since Peter the Great, becoming dangerously Westernized.

Westerners took Europe as their norm. They believed that Russia was a backward Western country, but that its youthful energy would give it advantages as it took its place among the European powers. Their intellectual justification for asserting this was Hegelian: that each nation had its place in the evolution of universal history, a period when its characteristics were dominant. In this scheme, the French period was coming to an end, the German period was beginning, but it would be succeeded by a period when Russia would take over. This evolutionary timetable assumed that Russia was becoming a nation, and that state and nation were mutually reinforcing – a dubious assumption for a multi-ethnic land empire.

The Crimean War

After the defeat of Napoleon, Russia became incontestably the leading land power in Europe. As other European countries set up constitutional political systems, though, Russia's autocracy began to seem anachronistic and even immoral. When it suppressed the Polish rising of 1830–1 and assisted the Habsburgs in suppressing the Hungarian rising of 1849, Russia became widely known as the 'gendarme of Europe'. Russian émigrés were reinforced by Polish ones in spreading ominous accounts of the despotic brutality of its rulers.

The origins of the Crimean War in the 1850s exemplified many of the problems which could arise from mutual misunderstandings between Russia and the European powers. Even after Russia conquered the northern shore of the Black Sea, its merchant navy – let alone its Black Sea Fleet – could still not be sure of free access to the Mediterranean, since every ship had to pass through the very narrow Bosphorus straits, which were controlled on both shores by the Ottoman Empire. The fate of that empire thus mattered vitally to Russia. By the mid-19th century, Turkey was widely regarded as the 'sick man of Europe', which had failed to reform fundamentally and hence was likely to collapse in the near future. Russia would welcome such collapse – but only if it could replace Turkey as ruler of Constantinople and fulfil the symbolic mission of restoring the cross to the great church (currently mosque) of Hagia Sophia. If, however, Turkey was supplanted by another European power, that power would offer an even greater threat to Russia than the Sultan's moribund realm. As Foreign Minister Nesselrode wrote in 1830:

> If we have allowed the Turkish government to continue to exist in
> Europe, it is because that government, under the preponderant
> influence of our superiority, suits us better than any of those which
> could be set up on its ruins.

A weak Ottoman Empire as Russian protectorate was far from
being the worst option.

Russia, then, vacillated between trying to destroy the Ottoman
Empire and trying to preserve and dominate it. In general, Russia
endeavoured to avoid war, especially against other European
powers, because war disrupted its finances and frequently also
generated internal unrest. In the meantime, it pushed for
maximum peaceful influence inside Ottoman territory by
reasserting its right to intervene on behalf of Christian subjects –
some 40% of the Ottoman population – quoting an obscurely
worded 18th-century treaty. Other European powers, especially
France, pressed to have similar rights acknowledged.

In 1844, Nicholas I visited Britain to consult about arrangements to
be made in case of Ottoman collapse. He proposed that Russia
should take land in the Balkans and Caucasus, place a garrison on
the Bosphorus, and declare Constantinople a free city, while Britain
would gain Egypt, and Austria the western Balkans. Nicholas left
London thinking that he had reached a 'gentleman's agreement' with
Palmerston. Actually, though, British statesmen construed Russian
aims as naked imperial expansionism, and their view was supported
by press and parliament, which were increasingly Russophobic. The
resulting distrust did a great deal to ensure that further disputes
over the Holy Places in Palestine led to outright war in 1853–4.
During that war, Britain did its utmost to destroy the Black Sea
Fleet, and to detach from Russia the Caucasus, Finland, the Baltic
provinces, and Poland – thus aiming at the obverse of Russia's
grandiose imperial objectives. Such were the outsize hopes and fears
which surrounded Russia's position in Europe.

The whole Crimean crisis showed that the vague and portentous diplomacy, the obsession with strength and status, the appeal to religious sentiment, and the attempt to gain potential allies on an adversary's territory, all of which had served Russia well in dealing with Eurasian steppe opponents, generated alarming and destructive crises when applied in Europe. They actually undermined the peace and stability which Russia generally sought to promote.

The Crimean War also demonstrated vividly the strengths and weaknesses of the Russian army. In areas that required the straightforward application of traditional technology, such as artillery and engineering, it performed well. Indeed, the rapid construction of the Sevastopol fortifications under General Totleben was a remarkable feat which denied the allies swift victory and compelled them to toil for a further year. Again, where simple operations required courage, comradeship, and the capacity to improvise, Russian soldiers had no superiors in Europe. These were the qualities which had enabled the Russian army to wage war so successfully throughout the 18th and early 19th centuries.

Now, in the mid-19th century, however, more was required. Both men and especially officers were woefully under-trained. Immaculate parade-ground discipline was no substitute for informed leadership in the field, backed up by competent staff work. Senior officers were still usually courtiers without specialist professional training. Transport and communications remained primitive, and the troops were poorly provided with food, clothing, and medical equipment. The absence of railways was especially felt. Britain and France were able to move troops thousands of miles across the sea more quickly than Russia could a few hundred miles across country. This defect was fatal in such a vast empire. Most of the Russian army never even reached the Crimea: it was guarding the Baltic coastline to prevent enemy landings, or was stationed in Poland and the Caucasus to prevent rebellion. The Russian army was the largest in Europe, but it could not be brought to bear on strategically decisive locations.

Besides, it was so large because it was inflexible. By this time, most nations had trained reserves they could mobilize if war threatened. But for Russia to mobilize serfs – who in any case were untrained – was dangerous to internal security. As the Napoleonic War had shown, mobilized serfs expected to be freed, and could become rebellious if they were not. That meant that in peacetime Russia had to keep its full standing army under arms and ready for combat – a hugely expensive burden, which crippled state finances.

This accumulation of problems helps to explain why a new Emperor, Alexander II (r. 1855–81), who came to the throne in the middle of the Crimean War, at last resolved on radical reform.

Chapter 4
The responsibilities and dangers of the empire

By the mid-17th century, it had become clear that Russia was primarily a north Eurasian empire, rather than an Orthodox ecumene or an embryonic nation-state. The way in which it acquired and extended that empire illustrates the strengths and weaknesses of Russia's geopolitical situation. It expanded to fill a vacuum which was both alluring and threatening. In Siberia, after defeating the Khanate in 1582, it faced only weak tribes, some of whom put up vigorous resistance, but none of whom could face down Cossacks equipped with firearms. Sweeping them aside, Russia expanded eastward all the way to the Pacific and became the largest territorial empire on earth, with immense resources. The exploitation of them, however, was hampered by the sheer size and remoteness of the territory.

The tools of imperial policy varied over time. In the 16th and 17th centuries, priority was usually given to suppressing any lingering resistance, then ensuring the integration of populations and making them loyal to the Tsar, whatever their internal arrangements, customs, and beliefs might be. This was usually achieved by co-opting the indigenous elites as local chieftains or religious leaders under the Tsar's ultimate authority. In the 18th and early 19th centuries, attention gradually shifted to bringing 'civilization' to non-Russian peoples, together with religious toleration and more direct administrative control. In the late 19th and early 20th centuries, serious disagreements began to arise among imperial officials. Some of them aimed to inculcate *grazhdanstvennost* (civic consciousness) among non-Russians, to give them a feeling of pride in belonging to the empire and political identification with it. This implied preserving non-Russian culture, but reducing it to an auxiliary and folkloric status. Other officials considered this policy dangerous, likely in practice to strengthen non-Russian cultural and political movements; they preferred to stick to more authoritarian methods, to emphasize administrative integration, and to encourage indigenous populations to convert to Orthodoxy and to adopt the Russian language for all public business.

These policies were pursued in different ways in different regions. In the Volga region, the first non-Russian territory to be conquered, in the 1550s, the Muscovite authorities at first tried to convert the Muslim Tatar elites to Orthodoxy. However, they soon abandoned this policy, judging it was likely to produce effective leaders of popular resistance and thus threaten internal security. All the same, they periodically resumed conversion campaigns, extending them further down the social scale. Priests and local officials went around the mostly pagan Chuvash, Mari, Mordvin, and Udmurt villages, driving their inhabitants down to the river to be baptized. The results, however, were superficial: by and large, the populations continued their previous observances. In places, moreover, the policy aroused serious turbulence, and the authorities eventually abandoned it.

Central Asia

In Central Asia, the main priority became vacuum-filling. During the 18th and early 19th centuries, Russia gradually pushed its defence lines southwards and eastwards into the steppe land of the Kazakh Hordes. The Kazakhs had themselves appealed to the Tsar for protection against invading Kalmyks from further out.

Russia complied willingly. Its motives were articulated by Foreign Minister Gorchakov in the mid-19th century:

> The situation of Russia in Central Asia is similar to that of all civilised states which come into contact with half-savage nomadic tribes without a firm social organisation. In such cases the interests of border security and trade relations always require that the more civilised state have a certain authority over its neighbours, whose wild and unruly customs render them very troublesome. It begins by first curbing raids and pillaging. To put an end to these it is often compelled to reduce the neighbouring tribes to some degree of close subordination.

Dealing with Kazakh nomads was easier if Russia could exercise some degree of authority over them, make them more dependent on Russian trade, and adapt their laws and customs to the needs of Russian officials and traders. Kazakhs welcomed Russian protection but sporadically rebelled against this incorporation into empire.

Until the mid-19th century, most of the Russian inhabitants of the steppe were Cossacks in mixed ranching and military settlements. From the 1870s onwards, increasing numbers of peasants came from the depressed central provinces of Russia, driven by the desire to create a better life for themselves. The Kazakhs at first tolerated this diminution of their pastures in the interests of the security the Cossacks afforded them. With the Resettlement Act of 1889, the state began systematically to survey and allot land to incoming settlers, whose numbers thereafter increased markedly. Their holdings began to cramp the nomads' movements and thus compelled them to take up a more settled life. Landholdings became more strictly delineated, disrupting inherited notions of land and property.

Between the 1860s and 1880s, the Russians conquered the Khanates of Kokand (which controlled the fertile Ferghana

Valley), Khiva, and Bukhara. The latter two became protectorates, while the first was abolished and Russian military rule was installed. By now, Russia was adopting a more pervasive method of imperial rule: imperial officials were brought in at higher and medium levels, while only the lower levels of authority were left to native headmen.

It was one thing to operate such a system within a culture familiar to all those intermediate administrators, quite another where the laws, customs, religion, and language were alien to them. Moreover, most Russian officials were military men, whose training ill fitted them to empathize with locals. Very few of them had even an elementary knowledge of local languages; they had to rely on indigenous interpreters, who were embedded in local networks and, undetected, could offer biased translations of the kind their colleagues wanted to hear. Russian officials guessed what was going on, but could do little about it. Such mismatches bedevilled many aspects of life: tax-collection, irrigation control, the administration of justice, and the settlement of disputes over religious endowments.

There were special difficulties when imperial concepts of law, custom, or hygiene differed markedly from those of locals. Among the Kazakh nomads, for example, the custom of *barimta* was widespread: it was considered honourable and proper, when other means of settling clan conflicts had failed, for one clan to take cattle, or even abduct a woman, to be returned when a settlement was finally reached. To Russian officials, this was theft or kidnapping, a criminal offence. Yet it was difficult to outlaw it without having anything effective to put in its place as a means of mediation.

The difficulties were intensified by the fact that Russian officials themselves disagreed on the ultimate purposes of their rule. General Kaufman, the first Governor-General in Tashkent, had long experience of the Caucasus, loathed Muslim 'fanaticism', and gave absolute priority to establishing good order as that was understood by senior army officers. In the long term, he expected Turkestan to evolve into an orderly, law-abiding region, but thought he could expedite the process by marginalizing Islam as far as possible. Many civilian officials, on the other hand, were committed 'Westerners', who believed Russia had a civilizing mission and aspired – like many of their counterparts in British India – to enhance the welfare of their colonial subjects and gradually turn them into full citizens of the Russian Empire. Such an outlook entailed tolerating Islam, allowing the ulema to continue their role, while gradually 'enlightening' them in the ways of the modern world, as interpreted by Russia.

The relative peace of Central Asia lasted only as long as the state's demands on its inhabitants were not too importunate. But in the middle of the First World War, when Muslims were for the first time conscripted to serve in the army, long-pent-up resentment exploded. There were riots in most major towns, and the army had to be called in to quell them. The loss of life and subsequent emigration into China meant that Turkestan lost nearly one-fifth of its inhabitants in 1916–17.

Poland and the western regions

When Russia annexed a large part of Poland in the late 18th-century partitions, it took on two peoples who were to prove especially irreconcilable to Russian rule: Poles and Jews. Poles formed the local elites, but the majority of the population were Ukrainians and Belorussians, long ago separated from Rus by the Mongol invasion. Imperial Russia felt a special right to incorporate them as part of the 'gathering of the lands of Rus'. But the Poles had alternative ambitions for them, as the subject population of the Polish-Lithuanian Commonwealth. That population was already partly Polonized: many belonged either to the Catholic Church, like the Poles, or to the Uniate Church, which practised Orthodox rituals but recognized the supremacy of the Pope. During the 1830s, they were forcibly converted to Orthodoxy, a campaign which left a legacy of bitterness among them.

Ukrainian culture itself became a tangible independent force inside the Russian Empire. Ukrainians claimed their distinctive political inheritance from the self-governing communities of the Cossack Hetmanate. In the early 19th century, Taras Shevchenko, freed from serfdom by an admiring patron, published *Kobzar*, a verse tale about a Ukrainian folk poet. It provided an example of how the various Ukrainian dialects might crystallize into a literary language. Later, Shevchenko was exiled for belonging to a society which aimed to convert Russia into a free federation of Slavic peoples. The government was seriously worried that Ukrainians, given their own literary language, might form a nation separate from Russia. Accordingly, in the 1870s publications and public performances in Ukrainian were banned.

Poles were much more difficult to assimilate. A proud people, with their own historical kingdom, high culture, and a more advanced economy, their elites bitterly resented Russian rule. They had their own distinctive experience of nationhood, and it included Ukrainians and Belorussians. Many Poles fought alongside Napoleon in 1812. Afterwards, Alexander I, seeking the best way to keep Poland loyal, experimented with a constitutional regime there, which many hoped might be extended to Russia as a whole. In 1830–1, however, the Poles rebelled and tried to throw off Russian rule altogether, and they repeated the attempt in 1863–4. The Polish nobles never had the convinced support of their own peasants, however, and both risings were suppressed, with considerable bloodshed. After the second, Poland's separate institutions were finally abolished. Poland was placed under martial law, many of its nobles and clergy were exiled to Siberia, and it became 'the Vistula region' of Russia. Meanwhile, Polish exiles in Paris, London, and elsewhere agitated in favour of a restored Polish kingdom, and gave Russia a bad name throughout Europe.

The 18th-century Polish partitions also brought some half a million Jews into the empire. They had an ancient religion and culture, a level of literacy and communal cohesion far higher than Russians; many of them also excelled in trade or one of the professions. Most of them were poor but, because they lived in compact ghettos or *shtetls*, they were regarded with suspicion and resentment by many in the local population, who feared their competition or exploitation. The government also worried that Jews would ruin Russian peasants if they were allowed to move freely, and so it mostly confined them to a Pale of Settlement in the western regions. By the May Laws of 1882, Jews were forbidden to own agricultural land even there. They were denied votes in the *zemstvos* (see below, p. 73) and municipalities, and numerical limits were placed on their admission to educational institutions. Deprived of the benefits of empire-wide trade and barred from agriculture, most of them remained poor, leading a marginal existence as shopkeepers, publicans, artisans, and stewards.

At times of crisis and unrest, as in 1881 and 1905–6, the Jews who lived in the cities of the Pale became targets for popular resentment. Russian or Ukrainian mobs would storm Jewish stores and workshops and assault their owners or anyone who looked Jewish. Many of the police had more sympathy with the rioters than with their victims, and were in any case swamped by the sudden violence. In the city worst affected, Odessa, some 800 Jews were murdered in 1905–6. Disgracefully, Nicholas II allowed his portrait to be carried by the Union of Russian People, a political organization which instigated anti-Jewish pogroms. He also blocked attempts to emancipate the Jews and repeatedly pardoned those found guilty of anti-Jewish violence.

The Baltic

When Peter I conquered the Baltic regions in the early 18th century, he confirmed the privileges, laws, and self-governing corporations of the local landed elites, who were German. He had good reason for doing this: they were excellent administrators. Many of them had been educated in German universities in 'cameralism' (public administration) and had experience of running corporate institutions on Western models. The huge and backward Russian Empire offered them far greater scope for exercising their skills than the petty principalities of Germany. At the same time, there was in the Baltic region no mass German population whose ascendancy to nationhood they could lead; hence they were dependent on empire for their dominance. Over the next two centuries, they not only ruled the Baltic, but provided numerous high officials for the administration of the entire empire, and for command in its army. For them, loyalty to the Emperor paid off: they were allowed to preserve their own culture and religion, and they retained tight control over the indigenous Estonian, Latvian, and Jewish populations.

Only in the 1880s did the Russian government endeavour to assimilate the Baltic barons to Russian nationhood, by introducing Russian administrative language, Russian-style municipalities, law courts, and schools, and building Orthodox cathedrals. In 1893, the German Dorpat University was closed and re-opened as a Russian establishment, Iuriev University.

Estonians and Latvians were already among the most literate peoples in the empire, thanks to their Lutheran religion. In 1905–6, their growing national consciousness produced a massive and violent movement of social and ethnic protest against Russians and Germans, in which both workers and peasants were involved. Russian punitive detachments restored order with even greater bloodshed. Thus, on the eve of 1917, the Baltic region simmered with discontent.

Finland constituted a very special case. Conquered from Sweden during the Napoleonic Wars, it remained a distinct Grand Duchy whose 'grand duke' was the Tsar. Otherwise, it had its own administrative system, and from the mid-19th century its own

Diet and its own army. Russian proponents of assimilation and administrative coordination found this both anomalous and dangerous, especially since the Finnish border was so close to St Petersburg. In the 1890s, the imperial regime embarked on a programme of complete integration of Finnish institutions, including army and Diet, into the imperial hierarchy, operating in the Russian language.

The Finns responded with a petition signed by no less than one-fifth of their population and then with a boycott of all Russian institutions. Conscripts evaded recruitment and went into hiding, protected by their countrymen. Russia found this peaceful resistance more difficult to cope with than violent rebellion, which it could always crush. In 1905, faced with rebellion throughout the empire, Nicholas II gave way and restored Finland's autonomous status.

The Caucasus

By the late 18th century, Russia had finally conquered the north coast of the Black Sea and begun to mobilize the abundant agricultural and commercial potential of the southern Ukrainian plains. The whole Caucasus and Transcaucasian region became an area of vital strategic interest, as a buffer zone against the Persian and Ottoman Empires. It was, however, exceedingly problematic territory, depicted in Greek mythology as the edge of the world. Peoples of very different lifestyles, ethnic origin, languages, and religions lived close to one another, though often separated by towering mountain walls. Some were traders, some transhumant nomads, some cultivators of vineyards and olive groves, some warring mountain tribesmen regularly feuding with each other. Some lived in semi-feudal petty kingdoms, others in more loosely articulated tribal confederations.

South of the highest range, the medieval Christian kingdom of Georgia, surrounded by Muslim powers, had fragmented into numerous smaller principalities but was beginning to revive again, and looked to its Christian big brother Russia for protection. To offer it, in the late 18th century Russian engineers built the Georgian Military Highway across the Caucasian massif to send armed convoys southwards. That highway needed its own protection from the mountain peoples living along its course. Providing that protection involved Russian armies in a half-century of destructive and costly warfare. As far as possible, Russian administrators proceeded by gaining the allegiance of tribal elites, and by exploiting their conflicts with one another, as they had done elsewhere. For military reconnaissance and patrol work, they relied on Cossacks, operating from bases at first on the plains north of the Caucasus, then later in the highlands.

Increasingly, Russian strategy aimed to eliminate clans that opposed them by mounting raids against them, destroying their habitat in the forests, then their settlements, and deporting them. This policy naturally aroused ferocious hostility against both the Russians and their native allies, especially in the eastern Caucasus, among the peoples of Dagestan and Chechnia. Resistance crystallized around the Sufi brotherhoods known as *tariqat*. Their adherents would adopt a discipline of silent prayer and meditation to prepare them for unyielding battle against the infidels. For several decades, they were led by a series of imams, of whom the most tenacious was Shamil, known as 'commander of the faithful'. He achieved unity by invoking Islam: his proclamations were directed against 'unbelievers' and 'hypocrites' rather than Russians as such. Under such leadership, the local tribes learned to suspend their feuds and unite to wage skilful and agile guerrilla campaigns, descending to storm Russian forts and outposts, then melting swiftly back into the mountains and forests. Slowly and painfully, the Russians devised a counter-insurgency strategy, but it was not till 1859 that they finally captured Shamil.

Even after that, resistance remained stubborn in the western Caucasus, among the Circassian people, who for centuries had lived as loose Ottoman vassals, secure in their upland fastnesses.

The Russians decided the only way to overcome their defiance was to physically displace them and resettle their lands with immigrants. In the end, during the 1860s, between one and two million Circassians were deported in appalling conditions to the Ottoman Empire, in whose successor territories their descendants still live today. This was the first great mass deportation of modern times. Russians achieved the mastery over the Caucasus at which they had aimed, but at the cost of alienating and embittering most of the peoples who lived there – a legacy that still has its destructive effects today.

Chapter 5
Reform and revolution

Reform

Defeat in the Crimean War removed the veto on radical change: it had become unavoidable. Russia had succumbed to two industrializing nation-states, and most reformers assumed that Russia must become one too, even though that required unsettling changes to its social structure. Westerners and Slavophiles had different conceptions of what was needed, but both felt it essential to give ordinary Russians a greater stake in the affairs of their country.

Above all, they both agreed on the need to abolish serfdom. Yet serfdom was the keystone of the empire's social and economic structure: removing it was extremely problematic. The dilemma was expressed by one landowner: 'To free the peasants without land is impossible, but to expropriate the landowners would be extremely unjust.' Not only unjust, but also unworkable, since one could scarcely deprive the ruling class of the principal source of its income. Yet peasants deprived of land would certainly not feel they had any stake in the system, and could easily become dangerously discontented.

The Emancipation Edict of 1861 was thus inevitably an unsatisfactory compromise. Landowners retained much of their land, especially in the south, where it was fertile and valuable. Peasants were awarded holdings which were usually smaller than those they had previously held; moreover, they were required to pay for land they thought they already owned in instalments over half a century. Nor were they set free as full citizens, but till they had paid off their debt were tied to a land commune, where as before joint responsibility was the norm. Since the landowner's administrative and judicial powers were abolished, those communes, and the purely peasant institution above them, the *volost* (township), gained more powers than they had ever possessed before. The *volost* court was to apply not statute law, but local custom as interpreted by peasant elders. Peasants thus remained a segregated social estate.

It is remarkable that such a far-reaching measure could be carried out at all in opposition to the interests of the ruling class. It was a vindication of the power of the much-criticized autocratic state, which alone could rise above the interests of all social classes.

One of the main reasons for abolishing serfdom was to create a non-serf army, in which all adult males would have the duty to serve, and in which a reserve could be built up without endangering rural security. War Minister Dmitry Miliutin pushed through that reform in the Military Conscription Act (1874), and insisted that all new recruits should take literacy classes. He also stipulated that officers should be professionally trained: he abolished the Cadet Corps and introduced so-called Junker Schools where non-nobles could qualify. After Miliutin left the post, however, the Cadet Corps were revived and literacy training was dropped. The chance to reforge the army as a 'school of nationhood', which is what Miliutin intended, was lost. Only in the First World War was that aim suddenly revived, but far too late to effect the necessary changes of mentality and organization.

The abolition of serfdom necessitated further reforms, to redistribute the functions which had previously belonged to the nobility. Local government was now entrusted to *zemstvos* and municipalities, elected assemblies dominated by the nobility and property owners, but with some representation from other classes, including peasants.

Other reforms were intended to create civil society on a 'Western' model. Censorship was eased, to facilitate open discussion of social problems. Education at all levels was expanded, and was opened to all social estates. Most controversial of all, the judicial system was totally reformed. In criminal cases, trained lawyers were to represent the accused, while juries drawn from ordinary citizens and peasant officials would decide the verdict. Proceedings would be open to the public and the press, and judges were to be independent and irremovable. In a sense, this was the first serious limitation on autocracy, since it implied that law, as determined by courts, was the highest authority – that laws in fact were written for governments as well as for subjects. It was certainly difficult to combine it with autocracy, as a sensational case demonstrated in 1878. Vera Zasulich, a young revolutionary, shot and wounded General Trepov, Governor-General of St Petersburg. No one denied that she had attempted murder, but to applause in the courtroom, the jury acquitted her on the plea of her lawyer that she had 'no personal interest in her crime', but was 'fighting for an idea'.

Autocracy remained unchanged, however: as she left the courtroom, Zasulich was re-arrested. Furthermore, when Interior Minister Valuev proposed having elected *zemstvo* representatives in the State Council, the empire's highest advisory chamber, Alexander replied that he opposed a constitution, not because it would restrict his authority, but because it would lead to the dissolution of Russia. The recent Polish rising greatly troubled him; he feared giving non-Russian elites a serious voice in the empire's highest institutions.

A changing society

The effect of the reforms was to create a much more changeable and differentiated society. With the construction of railways (culminating in the Trans-Siberian, completed in 1903), communications improved greatly. Heavy industry, hitherto largely military, branched out into other fields, and consumer manufacture developed rapidly. Because of Russia's weak currency, though, its faltering rule of law, and its cumbersome procedure for setting up joint-stock companies, much industry was owned by foreigners. Russia was threatened with becoming economically colonized, like China or the Ottoman Empire.

The way was now open for peasants to become literate, to diversify their economy, to work in the towns, on the railways and rivers, to serve in the army, and then return to civilian life. A whole new class of professional people emerged (nearly all men), trained in higher or technical educational institutions, and working for the state, the *zemstvos*, or the armed forces as doctors, lawyers, teachers, accountants, and administrators. New newspapers and journals appeared, each trying to appeal to a broad and growing educated public; no longer was serious discussion confined to small circles of intellectuals. Public opinion (*obshchestvennost*) took shape for the first time as a force independent of direct state tutelage. Its members were now able to participate in local government and in the organization of their own professions, but they were still excluded from politics at the centre, nor could they be confident of the rule of law or the security of civil rights. The more frustrated and strident among them constituted a new sociocultural stratum, divorced from both state and people, the intelligentsia – a new concept which Russia gave to the world.

The result was a paradoxical state of affairs. Civil society and the state were both growing stronger simultaneously, but as opponents, not as partners. The state depended for its conduct of local affairs largely on the Ministry of the Interior and on the provincial governors and police officials subordinate to it. Those officials had a wide range of ill-defined duties: it has been estimated that each provincial governor had an average of 300 to 400 official papers to deal with every day. Unable to cope with the flood, he tended to rely on personal links to trusted subordinates, to senior officials in St Petersburg, and on his right of personal report to the Emperor. District police chiefs faced the same situation in miniature, with the governor as their highest reference point, and exercised their responsibilities with minimal regard for strict legality, since they knew that administrative instructions always had priority.

The 1860s reforms made the political system even less coherent. The provincial and district *zemstvos* had no institutional links either upwards, to the government, nor sideways to provincial governors and district police chiefs, nor downwards, to the purely peasant *volost*. The chairman of each *zemstvo*, the noble marshal, would of course get to know these officials personally and negotiate some kind of *modus vivendi*. But he too had a plethora of functions, and no staff to support him; moreover, he was unpaid. It is not surprising that local affairs were managed by improvisation and personal contacts.

From 1881, after the assassination of Alexander II (see below, p. 82), states of emergency were introduced to give governors and police chiefs expanded powers: they could suspend law courts and newspapers, prohibit meetings and impose administrative exile, to deal with whatever they identified as posing a threat to orderly government. In the attempt to plug some of the gaps in the 'power vertical', a local noble was appointed as 'land commandant' with a wide range of powers over *volosti* and village communes. The political police was strengthened but was never large enough to deal with the growing opposition; nor were its links with society strong enough to enable it to gather information readily about really menacing threats to security.

In the late 19th century, then, Russia had two parallel and largely unconnected systems of governance. The vacuum which had always existed between state and population became even wider and more dangerous. Civil society became stronger, but so also did the instruments of state repression. In those potentially explosive circumstances, since there was no parliament, the press became especially important.

Russian nationalism

In the press, the relationship between the state and the population was now the subject of relatively open discussion. The fundamental question was 'What is Russia?' The successful European countries were nation-states with a high degree of industrial and commercial development. Should Russia emulate them, and, if so, how?

The energetic and enterprising editor of *Moskovskie vedomosti*, Mikhail Katkov, had one answer. He had been a Westerner, an admirer of the British political system. But the 1863 Polish rising persuaded him that in a multi-ethnic society, a freedom-loving gentry could be a force for sedition. 'To give up Poland would deprive Russia of its political significance in Europe', and the Russian people of 'its world-historical mission'. Katkov's answer was to convert the Russian Empire into a Russian nation, all of whose peoples, whatever their ethnic identity, would acknowledge the Emperor as their sovereign, as the Welsh, Scots, and Irish did the British monarch. Alternative nation-building projects, like the Poles', would have to be crushed.

The problem with restricting the rights of non-Russians was that they aroused the resentment of many hitherto loyal non-Russian subjects without increasing Russians' sense of empowerment. In fact, Russians were beginning to feel that their nation was also being systematically disadvantaged in favour of foreigners – especially, as many of them saw it, Jews. This feeling culminated in 1905 in the formation of the Union of Russian People.

In some ways, Russian nationhood was strongly developed. Most Russians, including the uneducated, had a concept of 'Russia', which involved the Tsar, the Orthodox Church, Russian language and literature, and they shared a rich subculture of folklore, music, dances, woodcuts, and other entertainments. They celebrated saints' days and Russian military victories. But this cultural understanding of Russia had not taken shape in nationwide political institutions.

Russian culture

Russia's high culture was assuming some of the functions of those missing political institutions. Far-reaching, disruptive change was being introduced, to all appearances from outside, from a Europe to which Russia did not feel it fully belonged. The rule of law, capitalist economics, rationalism, technical progress, and the urban, bourgeois way of life all seemed alien to most non-Westernized Russians, especially to peasants and the church. In this respect, Russia was the first modern nation that reacted against Western-driven modernization to reaffirm the values of inherited communal and religious life.

Faced with these challenges, and with state and church censorship which obstructed open discussion of how to cope with them, prominent writers felt obliged to assume the role of oblique political commentators and even prophets. Nikolai Gogol first made his name in the 1830s with sketches of Ukrainian provincial life and folklore, but to advance his career he decided to move to St Petersburg. There, the frosty formality and pretentious hierarchy of imperial Russia repelled him, and he satirized it in a series of works. In his novel *Dead Souls* (1842), he manipulates the term 'soul', used officially to designate a poll-tax payer, and the administrative fiction that deceased taxpayers were considered alive till the next census. His main character creates fraudulent social status for himself by purchasing such 'dead souls' from impoverished landowners.

Dead Souls was intended to be merely the first part of a work in which Gogol would show how Russia could be redeemed by its innate virtues. He found the rest impossible to complete and secretly burnt the manuscript. Instead, he issued a series of epistles preaching repentance and submission to the will of God. His admirers were bitterly disappointed.

Fedor Dostoevsky was similarly obsessed with the loss of community and of moral consciousness in modern urban civilization. He reacted against the project of understanding human beings as wholly a product of scientifically ascertainable biological and psychological laws. His 'Underground Man' (1864) sticks out his tongue at the Crystal Palace and proclaims 'I dislike the fact that two times two makes four'. The St Petersburg Dostoevsky describes in his novels is a hive of Western rationality, bureaucracy, and avarice, where a lonely, rootless individual like Raskolnikov can decide it is legitimate to murder an elderly moneylender because her life is useless and without her money he cannot finance his studies. Against this nightmare morality Dostoevsky counterposed that of the village community, bound by joint responsibility and Orthodox Christianity: Russian peasants might be drunken and blasphemous, but they had preserved the humble faith and spirit of community which the West had long ago lost. He believed that by asserting their unassuming and pious morality, Russia would save humanity. He issued a regular newspaper column, in which he preached war for the conquest of Constantinople from the Ottoman Empire and the rebirth of the Second Rome as a Russian capital city.

Like Dostoevsky, Lev Tolstoy was a Russian patriot, but an idiosyncratic one. In *War and Peace* (1869), he maintained that

Russia managed to defeat Napoleon not because of its skilful generals, but because of the moral superiority of ordinary Russian peasants and soldiers, who in their villages and regiments had succeeded in preserving a primitive sense of community and morality which the sophisticated, atheist French had lost. He endeavoured himself to live a life close to that of the peasants, at one stage making his own boots and joining in the scything of hay. In later life, Tolstoy founded a religion based on the ethic of mutual cooperation and asserted that this was the central message of Jesus. He rejected both state and church, on the grounds that (whatever they preached) they practised materialism, domination, coercion, and latent violence. He advocated abstention from all war and the abolition of the death penalty, money, and private property.

In music, Modest Mussorgsky insisted that Russian opera should reflect the Russian way of life and that its melodies should derive from folksong, the liturgy, or the rhythms and intonation of Russian speech. In his operas *Boris Godunov* (1874) and *Khovanshchina* (1880), he put his ideas into practice. Both portray turning points in Russian history when Western and Russian culture clash, and when trust between rulers and ruled is at issue. At the end of *Khovanshchina*, Old Believers immolate themselves in their church, singing the native *znamenny* chant, while offstage Peter I's army approaches playing Western military music.

By the early 20th century, Russia's challenge to traditional forms and genres, especially in music and painting, was more radical than in any other European country, probably because the challenge to Russian society itself from urbanization and industrialization was more abrupt and testing than elsewhere. Russia led the way in formulating the techniques and aspirations of modernism, which usually claimed deeper insight into a spiritual or underlying reality not apparent to routine perception.

In *The Rite of Spring* (1913), Igor Stravinsky disclosed more primitive and pagan layers of peasant culture than any of the folklore revivalists of England, Hungary, or Romania. Drawing on ancient Russian folk dances, he portrayed fertility rites and human sacrifice through brutal rhythms and static, non-progressive harmonies, implying a cyclical view of time. *The Rite*'s first performance by the Ballets Russes in Paris scandalized audiences and signalled that a new kind of modernism had arrived in European art.

Visual artists inherited the ambition to transform the world. Vasily Kandinsky began from a fascination with Russian folk art and produced highly coloured pastiches of familiar popular motifs. He moved on from there to equally highly coloured abstract paintings, believing that by renouncing any attempt to depict objects realistically, he was liberating art from its imprisonment in the material environment, and creating 'moments of sudden illumination' which 'reveal with blinding clarity new perspectives, new truths'. In short, he held that abstract art enabled the viewer to penetrate the secrets of the spiritual world underlying perceived reality.

Kazimir Malevich's *Black Square* (1915) was the shape of an icon, but placed in a void where the iconic image should have been. It substituted for church dogma a realm of pure potentiality, opening the way in his view to an ideal cosmos where creative possibilities were endless. He followed it up with a whole series of paintings consisting of simple geometrical forms pierced by lines, planes, or other simple shapes. He chose the term 'Suprematism' for his kind of art. 'I have conquered the lining of the heavenly....Sail forth! The white free chasm, infinity is before us!'

Thus, before 1917, Russia's art forms portended radical change even more all-embracing than was envisaged by modernists in other European countries.

8. The vacant icon: Malevich's *Black Square*

Socialism

The intelligentsia had its own views of 'Russia'. Alienated from the state, many of them idealized the *narod* (people), even though their links with it were tenuous; hence they became known as *narodniki*. They adopted some Slavophile views, but gave them a much sharper anti-state orientation. The essence of Russia, they declared, lay in its peasant communes, with their democratic self-government, mutual aid, and periodic redistribution of assets. The peasants should now be given all the land, and Russia should become a federation of such communes, with minimal coordination and control from the centre. Endowed with 'land and freedom', the peasants' spirit of equality and resource-sharing would generate social harmony and release the productive forces of the people.

How, though, should this situation be brought about? Some socialists believed the first priority was to bring their ideas to the peasants, 'going to the people', like Christian missionaries in darkest Africa, to live among them and awaken them to the political significance of their own communal practices. Under this impetus, in 1873–4 several hundred young people, many of them students, abandoned their studies, learned a trade such as cobblery or joinery, donned rustic clothing, and set out for the villages. Some were heartened by what they experienced, but many of them felt out of place and misunderstood. They were, moreover, conspicuous figures in the rural milieu, and many of them were arrested, imprisoned, sometimes for years, then tried and sentenced for 'sedition'.

Other socialists thought such self-sacrifice futile: it was necessary first to fight the autocratic state, since while it existed, no progress could be made. During the 1870s, an organization calling itself *Narodnaia volia* (People's Will or People's Freedom) carried out a series of assassinations of senior officials. In March 1881, they succeeded in their ultimate goal, and murdered Alexander II himself as he was proceeding in his carriage through the streets of St Petersburg.

After his death, police repression dispersed the surviving members of the organization, but it revived in the late 1890s, now as the Socialist Revolutionary Party (SRs). It reacted to the growth of an industrial working class by postulating that the *artel* would play in the towns the same role as the commune in the countryside, as a forum for revolutionary activity. Workers and peasants would act together to overthrow the Tsarist regime.

By now, the SRs had a rival, in the form of a socialist party which was not interested in the peasant community, but proclaimed that Russia's revolutionary future lay in the hands of the urban working class. Inspired by the theories of Marx, the Social Democrats (SDs) asserted that capitalism, as it came from Europe

9. Patriarch Alexii sanctifies the monument to Tsar Alexander II, erected only after the fall of the Soviet Union

to Russia, would create an alienated proletariat which would ultimately rise and seize power. The party split at an early stage. One faction, the Mensheviks, believed in a mass working-class party which would form a parliamentary opposition during the 'bourgeois' stage of history. The other, the Bolsheviks, believed that parliaments were a sham, and advocated a small party of 'professional revolutionaries' which would lead the workers in a decisive uprising to prevent the bourgeoisie ever taking power. Vladimir Lenin, their leader, took over the *narodnik* notion that the peasants were a potentially revolutionary class. Given appropriate leadership, he asserted, they would join the workers and enable them to defeat the bourgeoisie.

The 1905 revolution

Ever since the early 17th century, popular rebellions had periodically shown that Russia's communities of joint responsibility, which the regime exploited for its own purposes, could also act as a forum for social unrest. Cossacks, non-Russians, and peasants were imperfectly reconciled with their status, and there were no intermediate institutions through which they could articulate their grievances. From time to time, they resisted discreetly, or even rebelled openly when they sniffed an opportunity.

With the rapid development of industry in the final decades of the 19th century, the conditions of popular unrest changed radically. During the second half of the 19th century, the various nationalities and social classes had been gradually drawn into an empire-wide social and political culture through the development of railways, military conscription, the spread of primary education and of newspapers. Many younger male peasants were now literate and had the experience of army life, factory labour, and travel on the rivers and railways. Some of them had come into contact with political ideas, on their journeys, through reading newspapers, or through the efforts of activists to reach them at their workplace. They had a fuller sense of how their own grievances and humiliations were experienced by others and of how they might act together to assert themselves as citizens and gain greater control over their own lives.

An urban working class appeared, concentrated in the largest cities. Many of them were peasants seeking new sources of income. When they came into the city, they would seek to create for themselves forms of social life familiar from the village. Many of them lived in *zemliachestva* (groups of workers from the same province) and worked in *arteli*, each with its own *starosta* (elder). They agitated to be treated politely by managers, that is, not as 'serfs', and to be allowed to elect worker representatives to mediate in disputes. SRs and SDs organized study circles, to teach workers the elements of socialism and give them experience of acting together to defend their interests. The government, however, regarded their demands, and the accompanying strikes and demonstrations, as political subversion.

The first mass workers' movement was mobilized by an activist priest, Gapon, with the tacit support of the Metropolitan of St Petersburg. Gapon believed it would be best if the workers achieved their aspirations to civil freedoms and political participation through the action of the Tsar. He organized a workers' demonstration in St Petersburg in January 1905 to present a loyal petition. The demonstrators requested the right to strike and to have a permanent committee of elected worker representatives in the factories. They also made political demands, for a constituent assembly and the rule of law. Unaccustomed to facing this kind of mass protest movement, the government got cold feet and at the last moment tried to ban the march, which went ahead anyway. Poorly briefed troops panicked, fired on the procession, and killed at least a hundred people.

News of the massacre, immediately dubbed 'Bloody Sunday', spread rapidly throughout Russia. Its resonance was especially powerful because most Russians, whatever they thought of their local bosses, regarded the Tsar as a benign 'little father'. It prompted a surge of violent discontent among most social classes and ethnic groups. The socialist parties became involved in many of the protests, helping to organize them and give them political direction, but the demands being put forward were similar everywhere and derived from the universal desire for civil freedoms, greater self-government, and participation in politics both locally and at the centre. Peasants met in their village assemblies, and discussed national politics, sometimes with the assistance of a schoolteacher or political activist. Then they drew up petitions, still mostly couched in terms of loyalty to the Tsar. At the top of their list was the demand for an end to private landed property and the transfer to them of all non-peasant land, to be administered by their own communities. As a village in Vladimir province declared, 'Land must not be a thing that can be traded. It must belong to the people, so that everyone has access to it and everyone can apply his labour and live off it.' Then came demands for fairer taxation, universal free primary education, full civil rights, and a legislative assembly elected by all the people. What this amounted to was completing the agenda of the 1860s reforms.

The demands of workers were very similar, since, after all, many of them were peasants working away from home, and even those who were not felt a common sense of oppression. Understandably, they showed greater concern for political rights and somewhat less for questions of land tenure; and they had specific demands, such as the eight-hour working day, the right to strike, 'normal' wages, and the right to participate in factory management.

Altogether, the demands of workers and peasants showed how far ordinary Russians had advanced towards an understanding of general political problems and felt entitled to participate in their solution. No less remarkable were their modes of self-organization and action in 1905–6. They based themselves on their traditional collectivities to devise new forms of association and direct – sometimes violent – action. Peasants met in their village assemblies to consult on the most appropriate steps: some decided to harvest the landowner's crops, fell his timber for their own use, or graze their cattle on his meadows; some refused to provide labour for his estate; some went further and raided the manor house, taking everything they could use and expelling the owner, then in many cases burning down the house so that he could not return. Usually they insisted on acting unanimously and together, so that if the authorities re-established control, they could not single out ringleaders.

Industrial workers called meetings first of all at factory level, but then in many cases elected delegates to a city-wide 'Council of Workers' Deputies' – a soviet – to decide whether a general strike was needed, to organize it if so, and to take over municipal government while it lasted. Here, at enthusiastic but stormy meetings, held in a large hall or even on a river bank, workers thrashed out a common policy together. This was the closest to direct democracy that could be implemented in practice: all workers usually had the right to attend soviet meetings, to speak if not to vote, and to recall their delegates if they proved unsatisfactory. The largest soviet, that of St Petersburg, chaired by SD Lev Trotsky, ordained a general strike in October 1905 which quickly spread to other cities. It was decisive in forcing the Tsar to make serious political concessions.

Soviets were effective, then, in channelling workers' desire for resolute action. But they had a serious downside. Village assemblies worked well because they were reasonably compact. Urban soviets were huge and chaotic affairs, products of improvised organization in a crisis, and difficult to convert into stable institutions. That made it easy for demagogues or well-organized political parties to take them over – a fateful weakness, as we shall see, in 1917. Here the absence of in-between associations mediating between people and government made itself painfully felt.

The State Duma

Under pressure from the revolution, in October 1905 Nicholas II launched much the most ambitious attempt yet to create an institutional link with ordinary people. In the October Manifesto, he announced the creation of a State Duma, a legislative assembly to be elected by a multi-stage procedure which included most of the adult male population but gave more direct representation to urban and rural elites. In future, the Manifesto pledged, no law would take effect without the Duma's consent. This promise patently limited the Tsar's powers, but nevertheless in the fundamental laws which gave shape to the new politics, he was still referred to as the 'autocrat'. Besides, an upper house, the State Council, was placed alongside the Duma; half of it was to be appointed by the Tsar, while the other half was dominated by the nobility. An air of ambiguity surrounded the new politics from the outset: was this an autocracy or a constitutional monarchy?

The appearance of the Duma stimulated the formation of political parties as a link between the population and their representatives. Socialist parties were able to leave the underground and organize legally to contest elections. Professional people were best represented by the Constitutional Democratic (Kadet) party, which favoured a parliamentary government, radical land reform, and far-reaching autonomy for the nationalities.

The Duma might have become an effective intermediary between government and people if the workers, peasants, and non-Russian nationalities had felt that it gave them a reliable means of feeding their views into the political arena. They tried to treat it as such: mass participation in the first elections in 1906 was very high. The result was a Duma whose majority put forward the kind of programme one would expect from peasant petitions, with the demand for radical land reform in pride of place. The government set its face against this demand, and dissolved the Duma before it had lasted three months. A Second Duma, elected in the same way, gave similar results. It seemed as if the outcome of the abrupt experiment with a popular legislative assembly was to be a fruitless confrontation between it and the regime.

The government dissolved the Second Duma too. That might have been the end of the Duma as an institution. But government had also been strengthened by the creation of the post of prime minister. Its holder, Petr Stolypin, had a broader political vision: he insisted the Duma should continue, though with a reduced franchise, which gave the dominant position to landowners, urban elites, and Russians; some non-Russians lost their voting rights altogether. His intention was to strengthen the monarchy by providing it with an institutional base among the empire's elites and thus create a political Russian nation.

As part of his plan, Stolypin endeavoured to release peasants from the village commune and make them full citizens, in order to promote modern commercial farming and create a politically loyal class of small landed property owners. The Third Duma passed his reform. But the distance between the state and the people was revealed yet again. Stolypin's vision foundered on a complex and many-faceted rural reality. Most peasants, even if they wished for more freedom to engage in the market, still needed to participate in the decisions of their village community, and still wanted the security provided by the communal safety-net. Many villagers passively or actively resisted the claims of those who wished to separate their land from the commune's, usually because separation disrupted communal arrangements (for crop cycles or pasturing livestock, for example) and threatened to restrict the freedom the commune still enjoyed to redistribute land periodically according to its own criteria. Even where wholesale retitling and enclosure of the land was carried out, officials discovered that communes continued to govern many aspects of land use as before.

Stolypin soon found himself in a hard place between the Duma and the Tsar. Nicholas had granted the October Manifesto reluctantly and hankered after downgrading the Duma once the revolutionary movement had subsided. He was supported by many courtiers. At the same time, the nobility, using their bastion in the State Council, resisted Stolypin's other proposed reforms, which would have weakened their hold on local government and justice, the education system, and the armed forces. Stolypin, for his part, was murdered in 1911, in circumstances that have remained obscure.

The First World War

The engaged and articulate political public had greatly increased as a result of 1905. The number of newspapers and journals grew exponentially, and they attracted readers from social classes which the press had hitherto scarcely reached. Censorship was much weaker, so that considerably more information was now available, and controversial issues were discussed in a lively and accessible language. The result was that, when war broke out in 1914, politics had become much more raucous and confrontational than before 1905.

War nevertheless offered a last chance to create national unity. When it broke out, massive crowds flooded on to the streets to cheer the Tsar. The Duma voted war credits and then prorogued. *Zemstvos* and municipalities offered to take over medical care and other services for the army. 'Civil society' was being created in emergency mode.

The effect was not durable, however. Military defeat, notably the loss of Poland in 1915, faltering ammunition supplies at the front, food shortages, profiteering, and inflation in the rear all revived the pre-war confrontational mood, intensified now that so much was at stake. One result was the abrupt desacralization of the image of the monarchy. Nicholas's reputation, sullied by Bloody Sunday, was further damaged by military defeat – a crucial matter for a Tsar. Further damage was done by the disreputable antics of

Grigorii Rasputin, a Siberian sectarian 'holy man' who had wormed himself into the Empress's confidence by being able to staunch the bleeding of her long-awaited son, Alexei, who had haemophilia. Increasingly, Rasputin influenced court and even government appointments, exploiting his power to make sexual conquests among high society ladies. To the newspapers, the mixture of heresy and debauchery in high places proved irresistible, and the public was entertained with lurid tales about his behaviour. The fact that the Empress was German (a perfectly normal situation in royal families) compounded the widespread suspicion, even amongst the most loyal, that corruption and treachery were infecting the court.

In February 1917, demonstrations over food shortages combined with workers' grievances to bring hundreds of thousands on to the streets of Petrograd (as the capital had been renamed). Placards appeared demanding an end to the war and to autocracy. Politicians decided the time had come to demand Nicholas's abdication and sent a delegation to him at military headquarters. Most of the generals, whose priority was a united nation backing the army, concurred that Nicholas had become a liability. He duly abdicated in favour of his brother, Grand Duke Mikhail. The latter, dismayed by the anti-monarchical feeling in the capital, declined the throne.

The 1917 revolution

Russia was suddenly without a monarch, for the first time for three hundred years. Duma politicians set up a Provisional Government to head the war effort and plan reforms pending a Constituent Assembly, which would be elected to decide the future form of Russia's government. Immediately at its side appeared another institution, designed to represent the masses rather than the elites: encouraged by the political vacuum, the workers and peasants, now reinforced by soldiers and sailors, hastened to resuscitate their most effective political weapon of 1905, the soviets. The Petrograd Soviet was backed by a network of similar assemblies in towns throughout the empire. Workers also improvised a variety of other associations: trade unions, factory committees, and, in a growing number of towns, Red Guard militias, which acted both as custodians of civil order and as armed representatives of the working class. Never had the Russian genius for improvised collectives manifested itself so visibly – but not in a form which strengthened national unity. On the contrary, 'dual power' made visible the continuing split between elites and masses.

The soviets in a sense embodied the centuries-old popular drive towards social justice and self-government. Yet what had worked tolerably well in the villages was not so easy to transfer to the towns. The scale was so much bigger, and the problems to be tackled so much more complex. A Menshevik activist has left us a vivid depiction of the working of the Petrograd Soviet, where the crowd was so dense that everyone was standing rather than sitting:

> The 'presidium' was also standing on a table, while around the shoulders of the chairman was a whole swarm of energetic people who had clambered on to the table and were hindering him from conducting the session.

In such circumstances, little could be decided in plenary sessions, and responsibility inevitably devolved upon executive committees, where the socialist political parties were well represented. During the summer, as the masses became ever more impatient at the temporizing of the Provisional Government, the Bolsheviks gained ground in soviets throughout the country.

Peasants largely repeated their initiatives of 1905–6, only now with much greater impact, since the forces of law and order had crumbled. At first, peasants hoped the Provisional Government would transfer all land to them, but they became disillusioned at the slow progress it was making. They also became radicalized as soldiers deserting from the front returned to their homes with hopes of a forceful solution. During the late summer and autumn, village assemblies began to take drastic decisions, wherever possible by consensus. Typically, they would assemble with their carts on the village square, bringing weapons if they had them. They would make their way *en masse* to the local manor house, compel its owner to sign a document transferring the land to the village community, then load valuables onto their carts to take away with them. If the landowner cooperated, he would be assigned a plot of land on equal terms with the villagers; if he resisted, he would be deported or even murdered.

The February Revolution transformed the life of the army. One of the first acts of the Petrograd Soviet was to issue Order No 1, which mandated soldiers to elect committees to run units at company level and above. Theoretically, their responsibility was not to extend to actual combat, where officers retained their authority. This distinction was not always observed in practice, though, and in some units the men set about re-electing – or not – their commanders. To most officers, such insubordination was intolerable. One reflected ruefully in a letter:

> When we talk about the *narod*, we mean the nation; when they talk about it, they mean the democratic lower classes....We can find no common language: that is the accursed heritage of the old regime.

His comment reflected aptly the yawning division between *obshchestvennost* and masses in late Tsarist Russia: the former was creating a nation, the latter struggling for control of their own lives in communities of joint responsibility.

Soldiers were mostly prepared to go on defending Russia's borders, but they longed for peace, all the same, and were very concerned about their families and landholdings back at home in a period of upheaval and scarcity. In June, they began disobeying orders to undertake an offensive, and mutinies spread along the front. The same thing was happening in France, but there the government managed to restore order and discipline by appealing to the soldiers' republican patriotism. Such appeals were markedly less effective in Russia, where the army had never become a 'school of nationhood', and ordinary people felt much less committed to the political system.

Mutiny was followed by the gradual disintegration of the imperial army and the final breakdown of order in the rear as well. The Bolsheviks were well placed to take advantage of this situation. At this stage, they had no responsibility for the existing regime, or indeed for Russia's integrity as a state. They found it easy to appeal to workers, peasants, soldiers, and non-Russians: they could promise peace, land, bread, workers' control, national self-determination, and 'all power to the soviets' without considering the complexities of implementation. Their slogans resonated powerfully in the army and the larger industrial towns, but also caught on among the peasants.

The Bolsheviks gained majorities in most of the urban soviets, notably Petrograd, where in October, with the help of the Red Guards, they gained control of the city and expelled the Provisional Government. This was the great turning point which has gone down to history as the October Revolution. The Bolsheviks' seizure of power was conducted in the name of 'all power to the soviets'. But when Lenin appeared before the Second All-Russian Congress of Soviets, he announced he was creating a government, the Council of People's Commissars (*Sovnarkom*), consisting entirely of Bolsheviks. Most Mensheviks and many SRs refused to accept this usurpation of the popular mandate and walked out – thereby giving Lenin a free hand. The remaining SRs joined the Bolsheviks in a short-lived coalition, mainly on the grounds that the latter were proposing to satisfy the SR demand for immediate transfer of all land to the peasants.

In November, the long-awaited elections to the Constituent Assembly took place. The Bolsheviks performed respectably, but the SRs gained the largest number of seats. *Sovnarkom* accordingly closed the Assembly after only one session. The Red Guards then forcibly dispersed a workers' demonstration of support for the Assembly. The writer Maxim Gorky, himself a Bolshevik supporter, remarked bitterly 'The Petrograd workers were mown down unarmed by cowards and murderers....Do the "People's Commissars" not realise...that they will end up strangling Russian democracy altogether?'

It cannot be said, then, that the Russian people ever voted in their majority for the Bolsheviks. It was tragic that, in fighting for land, freedom, and self-government, the Russian communities of joint responsibility should have delivered themselves into the hands of an even more oppressive regime.

10. Lenin leaving an educational conference, 1918

The dissolution of the Constituent Assembly unleashed civil war between Reds and anti-Reds, usually known loosely as Whites. Faced with the collapse of central power, Russia disintegrated into local communities fighting for survival. The Whites were divided, as ever, by their visions of Russia. Some considered it a developing 'Western' country, where democracy and the rule of law would ultimately triumph, and so fought to re-establish the Constituent Assembly. Others opposed the Assembly as a hotbed of socialism and considered authoritarian rule essential; they fought for the reinstatement of 'Russia One and Indivisible'. It is striking that no White leader openly called for the restoration of Tsarism, so deeply was it discredited among ordinary Russians. All the same, the Bolsheviks murdered Nicholas II and his family, and threw their corpses down a remote mineshaft, so that their graves should not become shrines.

The Reds won the civil war largely because they had the support of many peasants, workers, soldiers, and non-Russian nationalities, because they occupied the central strategic position, and because they successfully projected their vision that they embodied the future. The Red Army, under the competent leadership of Trotsky, behaved no less brutally than the Whites, but operated more effectively. The experience of civil war left a lasting mark on the Bolshevik leaders: thereafter, they were in permanent mobilizational mode, seeing enemies everywhere and using the rhetoric of military campaigns to impel social change and economic development.

Chapter 6
The Soviet Union's turbulent rise

The 1917 revolution looked like a complete break with Russia's past. Yet before long the main features of that past had reappeared: empire, centralization, a highly authoritarian state, a yawning gap between rulers and people. How did this happen?

One unquestionably novel feature of the Soviet Union was rule by a single party, the Bolsheviks, who renamed themselves Communists (later the Communist Party of the Soviet Union, CPSU). Its leaders took over the messianism which had always been part of Russian religious culture and transposed it into politics, as the Tsars had never done. Communists believed that Marxism, as interpreted by Lenin, had given them the key to history and entitled them to a monopoly of power. They intended to defeat the class enemy, industrialize Russia, and join with the workers of other industrialized countries to foment world revolution and build communism throughout the world. To achieve this, they forged the party into a tightly centralized organism, directed by a self-perpetuating Central Committee and protected by a ubiquitous security police, the Cheka, later NKVD.

Their conviction that they were fighting for absolute good entailed the equally strong conviction that all their opponents represented absolute evil. In the civil war, they applied this belief to all anti-Reds, whether Russian nationalists, liberals, or non-Communist socialists. In their eyes, the struggle gave them the right not just to defeat but to exterminate their opponents.

The one-party system they established was a logical outcome of their world view. Unfortunately for them, it had a defect which initially appeared to enhance their power, but which ultimately proved fatal for them. Their monopoly of power over every aspect of public life enabled them in the early years to bring about change quickly and to deal with emergencies, but in the long run became rigid and irresponsive to the problems of the real world.

Among other things, it spawned a monopoly appointments system (*nomenklatura*). The party's rules stipulated that its members should strive to carry out party policy wherever they worked, and 'to exercise party supervision over the work of all organizations and institutions'. Responsible appointments in all walks of life required a resolution of the appropriate party committee. This meant that all factory directors, senior local government officials, headteachers, newspaper editors, and so on were vetted by their local party organization before appointment. For this purpose, party committees at all levels maintained a card index system listing all potential appointees to important posts and containing information on their qualifications, experience, and political reliability. When Joseph Stalin became General Secretary of the party in 1922, he perfected this system and used it to keep tabs on all his comrades and subordinates. Mao Zedong later said that power grew out of the barrel of a gun; but Stalin had already shown that it grew out of a well-kept filing cabinet. During the late 1920s and 1930s, he used it to defeat all his rivals and to rig show trials against many of them.

However, local party secretaries could and did manipulate this system too. Stalin could not keep a constant eye on the tens of thousands of party committees up and down the country. Their leaders used their own files to promote their own favourites. Thus, the party's power monopoly generated a hierarchy of patron–client

11. Portrait of Stalin by Isaak Brodskii, 1928

networks, whose grip on whole regions or branches of the
economy could be restrained only by extreme vigilance and
determined intervention from above.

Why, though, did organizational rivalries generate the grotesque
excesses of the 1930s terror? The Communist leaders were
profoundly marked by the experiences that had brought them to
power. They had endured privation together in the Tsarist

underground, sustained by their shared belief in their own mission. They had suffered arrest and exile, and fought a desperate civil war, which it often seemed they would lose. Their consciousness was formed by their awareness that they were surrounded by enemies and by popular indifference or hostility even while, as they saw it, they were trying to bring harmony and happiness to humanity. Through these abrupt changes of fortune, they forged intense interdependence and mutual trust, without which they could scarcely have persisted in their endeavour. Absolute trust in the party became a hallmark of Communists.

A warrior mentality coloured the Communists' responses to all social problems, including those of economic development. In their eyes, everyone but workers and the poorest peasants were potential enemies. In 1928, the state planning institution, Gosplan, launched the first of a series of Five Year Plans, intended to industrialize the country, replacing foreign capital with state allocation of resources. The plans were successful in increasing industrial output, but they required a net transfer of resources from the countryside to the towns. Offered lower prices for their crops, peasants responded by cutting their grain deliveries. The Communist leaders interpreted this market malfunction as deliberate sabotage by 'kulaks' – wealthier peasants who were 'class enemies'. They responded with two aggressive campaigns, implemented with military speed and thoroughness: 'dekulakization', and the creation of collective farms (*kolkhozy*), run by appointed officials, from which deliveries of produce could be enforced.

Plenipotentiaries were sent into the villages, with instructions to find out who the 'kulaks' were and to banish them from the communities. The most 'malicious elements' were deported to remote underpopulated regions of the north and Siberia, where they were dumped, often without suitable shelter, nutrition, or clothing. The peasants were then pressured into surrendering their land and livestock to *kolkhozy*, which were intended to bring industrial organization and discipline to agriculture. Some poorer villagers welcomed this, but the whole notion repelled most peasants, who were strongly attached to their household plots of land.

These measures brought about the destruction of the whole traditional rural way of life. Some peasants dubbed the results a 'second serfdom'. As more archive materials become available, historians have uncovered more and more cases of peasant resistance, often violent. Since the village church was usually closed as well and the priest arrested, some peasants actually believed that the reign of Antichrist had come, and that anyone who entered a *kolkhoz* would be 'branded with the stamp of the beast'.

In truth, both sides had apocalyptic expectations. Taken together with the industrial Five Year Plans, collectivization was the great and decisive struggle to create socialism. Lev Kopelev, a young activist at the time, confessed many years later:

> Stalin had said 'The struggle for grain is the struggle for socialism'.
> I was convinced we were warriors on an invisible front, waging war
> on kulak sabotage for the sake of grain needed for the Five Year
> Plan... [and] also for the souls of peasants whose attitudes were
> bogged down in ignorance and low political consciousness.

The destruction of the traditional village caused a major famine and poisoned the whole of social and economic life. The effects were especially devastating in Ukraine and Kazakhstan. Ukraine was a major grain-growing region: the campaign was conducted ruthlessly there, and became enmeshed with the suspicion that Ukrainians might favour treacherously leaving the USSR and joining Poland. Hence the '*holodomor*', the hunger-famine which many Ukrainians today judge a form of genocide. In Kazakhstan, collectivization entailed 'sedentarization', compelling nomads to adopt a settled way of life, which resulted in a catastrophic loss of cattle, and the death or emigration of a third of the population.

By the mid-1930s, many 'kulaks' managed to escape from their 'special settlements' and find jobs in the towns. Their appearance prompted a second spasm of terrorist activism by the state. In July 1937, Order No 00447 listed categories of 'socially harmful elements' to be arrested and, after a summary trial, either shot or sent to the Gulag. They included kulaks, priests, religious believers, old regime officials, and former members of non-Communist movements. The numbers to be arrested in each region were stipulated in advance; in practice, they were often exceeded as local NKVD agents 'worked towards' Stalin. In 1937–8, more than 760,000 people were arrested and 387,000 shot. Those who were not killed spent years, sometimes decades, in labour camps where exhausting work, poor nutrition, and inadequate medical care imposed their own death rates.

The manic distrust devastated party cadres too. Given his experience and mentality, Stalin could only interpret difficulties as a sign that enemies had infiltrated the highest levels of the party–state apparatus. The very intensity of the struggle had bred its own enmities, even – or perhaps especially – within such a tightly knit band of leaders. The struggle of black versus white left no room for shades of grey. After Lenin's death in 1924, each party faction struck a pose of absolute doctrinal rectitude and total moral authority. That meant that disputes over the best strategy tended to polarize opinion, transforming intense trust into intense distrust. Opponents and even waverers had to be treated as deadly enemies, to be attacked and destroyed. When the Central Committee worked out a particular strategy, it had to be adopted unanimously. Those who had reservations about it were accused of being 'deviationists', then of being 'oppositionists', which implied open hostility. Under such suspicion, Trotsky, Stalin's principal rival, was expelled from the USSR in 1929. In the 1930s, as the fear of war with Germany grew and social turmoil intensified, the rhetoric escalated further: 'oppositionists' became people with 'terrorist intentions', then full-scale 'terrorists' or 'enemies of the people', to be eliminated.

The *nomenklatura* system intensified these suspicions. Leading Communist officials in all regions defended their own trusted appointees from the prying eyes of the NKVD. Stalin became convinced that, as a result, 'terrorists' had ensconced themselves throughout the apparatus. He unleashed the NKVD on them. Between the 17th party congress in 1934 and the 18th in 1939, 110 out of 139 members of the Central Committee were arrested; of 1,966 delegates at the 17th, 1,108 had disappeared by the time of the 18th. In the most sensational cases, former party leaders, comrades of Lenin, were accused, at much-trumpeted show trials, of participating in a great conspiracy, directed from abroad by Trotsky, aimed at murdering the Communist leaders and colluding with foreign powers to restore capitalism in the USSR. Most of them confessed, under pressure from exhausting interrogations, threats to themselves and their families, and perhaps also the feeling that they could save themselves by rendering one last service to the party. They had given their lives to the conviction that history could be made only through the party, and they had no alternative beliefs on which they might make a stand or form an opposition.

Cultural and social policy

The Communists were utopians: they believed they could and should transform people's consciousness. Armed with the latest technology and with the only correct theory of social evolution, the 'new Soviet man' would be able to transform nature and build a more humane society. 'The average human type', Trotsky declared, 'will rise to the heights of an Aristotle, a Goethe or a Marx. And beyond this ridge new peaks will rise.'

How this was to be done was much debated during the 1920s. Proletkult, Constructivists, Futurists, and others with attractive Russian acronyms advertised their own nostrums for 'breaking down the barrier between art and life' – something they all agreed should be done. Mostly they were experimental and modernist, as seemed to befit a revolutionary culture.

By the 1930s, however, once the Soviet state was firmly established, the party aspired to dominate culture, as it did every other aspect of life. It no longer wanted innovative or 'revolutionary' artists: on the contrary, it favoured art forms which reflected the greatness and stability of the state, that is, a conservative, classical, easily appreciated style. In architecture, the pure straight lines and right angles of the international avant-garde gave way to voluptuous neo-Baroque motifs: sculpted banners, statues, and decorative friezes depicting the battles of the class struggle and the triumph of the workers. In the visual arts, abstraction and stylization were supplanted by simple genre scenes of everyday life or heroic tableaux of party leaders receiving the acclaim of an adoring public. In literature, experimentation and obscurity yielded to a sober, easily understood traditional realism, increasingly tending towards the optimistic and idyllic in its portrayal of Soviet life. In all the arts, this saccharine neo-conservatism was dignified with the title 'socialist realism'.

It was imposed through the *nomenklatura*-dominated organization of the arts. All professional cultural workers were enrolled in party-supervised 'creative unions', whose function was to take care of their material needs and ensure their access to the outlets they needed to bring their work to the public. The Writers' Union, for example, maintained a network of apartment blocks, holiday homes, and health resorts for writers' use; it also ran literary journals and publishing houses, and it negotiated contracts for writers. The journal editors played the key role in ensuring that what was published conformed to the ideology and taste of the party leaders. They consulted regularly with Writers' Union secretaries, with officials of the Central Committee cultural department, and with the state censorship, often negotiating minute and subtle changes to texts to render them acceptable.

This situation was ideal for technically competent, conformist writers. But for mavericks and the highly talented, it posed great

12. A contrast in architectural styles: (a) the constructivist Kharkov Palace of Industry

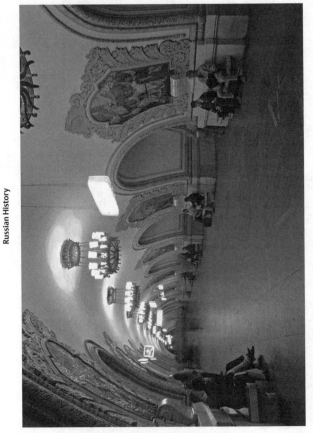

(b) the neo-Baroque Kievskaia Metro station

difficulties. They might want to fit into the new society, but they found it difficult to curb their own personal creative traits, which disconcerted the second-rate writers whose job it was to supervise them. Boris Pasternak devoted himself to translation; Anna Akhmatova wrote 'for the desk drawer'; Isaak Babel and Osip Mandelstam were arrested and died in labour camps.

Family policy likewise reverted to older values. Initially, the party had aimed to undermine the family, which in their view perpetuated inequalities and old-fashioned outlooks. They were especially anxious to free women from the duties of cooking, cleaning, and child care. In the 1920s, inheritance rights were curtailed, women's property rights were made equal to men's, *de facto* unions were considered as equal to registered marriages, abortion was available on demand, and a spouse could obtain a divorce by simply informing his or her partner.

It was soon discovered, though, that the state could not replace families in looking after children, old people, the sick, and disabled. Hundreds of thousands of orphans appeared on the street, begging and sometimes attacking passers-by or shops. The birth rate fell, which in the long term threatened both industrial development and the armed forces. Family legislation was not the sole cause of these problems, but nevertheless, Communists decided that it was important to have stable families to build socialism. Abortion was again virtually outlawed, and divorce was made much more difficult. Inheritance rights were restored, but only to the offspring of registered marriages.

One long-term problem remained from this compromise. In practice, women once again became responsible for the everyday duties of family life, which few men regarded as incumbent on themselves. Now, though, women were also expected to seek employment; for many, this was a necessity, since low rates of pay made it impossible to maintain a family on just one income. The result was that women were afflicted with a 'double burden', and often had to call in grandparents to help with the multiple demands on their time.

From the late 1920s onwards, millions of people were on the move, mostly from the countryside into the towns, either to get away from the *kolkhozy* or to find employment, often both. Since little extra housing was constructed, they had to crowd together in *kommunalki* (communal apartments), where a whole family might live in a single room, sharing kitchen, bathroom, and toilet with other families. The necessity to agree acceptable arrangements imposed a certain reluctant interdependence, a modified joint responsibility in subjection to the authorities (who allocated 'dwelling space'), which in exaggerated form replicated pre-revolutionary village experience. The lack of privacy created ideal conditions for informers, who sometimes made denunciations to the authorities to get rid of unwanted neighbours. Personal relations were decisive; there was no legal or institutional defence against abuse of power.

Work in Soviet enterprises also bolstered joint responsibility. All employees became part of a work team, subject to managers and foremen who had to ensure the fulfilment of Gosplan's targets and used collective discipline and collective rewards to achieve that. They had power not only over work practices, but often also over housing and social benefits. Everyone became part of a subordinate community, dependent on the bosses for life's essentials, with no effective individual rights.

National policy

Communist policy towards the non-Russian nationalities was very different from that of the Tsars. Communists believed that nationalism was a powerful but transitory sentiment, which could be harnessed for revolution, but which would in due course give way to a supra-ethnic all-Soviet consciousness.

Initially, the Communists utilized national identity as a way of promoting modernization. They created a federal state, with a hierarchy of ethnically named constituent republics, in which, at least theoretically, power devolved to indigenous elites trained for the purpose – a policy known as *korenizatsiia* (indigenization). The party specifically set out to encourage the development of non-Russian national languages and cultures. A campaign of *likbez* (liquidation of illiteracy) provided elementary education in local languages.

In principle, this was an enlightened policy, but from the outset it suffered from its own contradictions. First of all, given the intermingling of peoples throughout the former Russian Empire, designating a certain territory as belonging to a particular people entailed considerable over-simplification. Those who did not belong to a titular nationality felt discriminated against: local cadres tended to favour their co-nationals in housing, education, and employment. This sometimes handicapped Russians. In the Mordvin republic on the Volga, for example, 60% of the population was Russian, but their republic was named after a non-Russian minority. In Ukraine, many Russian parents bitterly resented their offspring having to study Ukrainian, which they considered a 'farmyard dialect'.

Besides, many Soviet practices directly undermined *korenizatsiia*. The party, the armed forces, and Gosplan were all tightly centralized, so that the non-Russians' scope for self-rule was in practice extremely constricted. In any case, during the 1930s, the practical application of *korenizatsiia* was changed. Internal passports were introduced, in each of which 'entry no 5' designated an individual's nationality. The entry could not be changed, and it gradually became a more important determinant of life chances than social origin.

Moreover, since no socialist revolutions had occurred elsewhere, commitment to world revolution now implied defending Russia at all costs: 'Socialism in One Country', as Stalin called it. During the 1930s, party propaganda increasingly emphasized the Russian identity of the Soviet Union as a whole. The Tsars were no longer condemned outright as exploiters of the people, since their conquests had created the great state which was now the Soviet Union. Stalin declared:

> We have inherited that state ... [and] have consolidated and strengthened it as a united and indivisible state, not in the interests of landowners and capitalists, but for the benefit of the workers, of all the peoples who make up that state.

Schools in all republics were required to teach the Russian language. Russian literature, especially Pushkin and Tolstoy, was extolled as the standard for all Soviet writers to emulate. Ethnic units were abolished in the Red Army, and Russian was made the universal language of command. Many nationalities were required to reformulate their written languages using the Cyrillic alphabet. The Soviet peoples were still in principle equal, but the Russians were definitely 'more equal' than the others.

Actually, though, this was imperial and not ethnic Russian-ness. It envisaged the Russians primarily as the bearers of a great state. Stalin had little interest in the ethnic customs of the Russian people, which were being destroyed even as the new Russification took hold. In particular, the Russian village commune and the Orthodox Church were being deliberately undermined as an objective of Communist policy.

Soviet educational and economic policies transformed the consciousness of all nationalities, including the Russians. Mass primary education and *likbez* produced a generation of young people, literate in their own language, and at the same time becoming urbanized. This was the Soviet Union's greatest long-term achievement. At the beginning of the Second World War, the average Russian Red Army soldier was far more aware of his national traditions than his counterpart only a quarter of a century earlier. But the same was true of non-Russians: thus, the Ukrainians who sought urban employment during the 1930s–1950s were nationally aware, and transformed what had been Russian, Polish, and Jewish towns into Ukrainian ones, centres of a conscious Ukrainian culture.

As the threat of war grew during the 1930s, Stalin perceived some nationalities as potentially treacherous. Poles and Germans were deported from areas near the western borders. In 1937, when Japan invaded China and seemed to threaten the Soviet Union, all Koreans were deported from the Far East. This was not just removal from a sensitive region: after they reached their destinations, Koreans were forbidden to attend Korean-language schools or to read Korean newspapers. For the first time, the Soviet authorities were endeavouring to extirpate the cultural existence of a whole nationality.

They continued such policies during and after the war. As they occupied eastern Poland and the Baltic republics under the terms of the Nazi–Soviet Pact of 1939, they deported many local elites – anyone capable of organizing national resistance – to Siberia and Kazakhstan. In the Polish case, this was accompanied by the deliberate mass murder of some 20,000 army officers and professional people. In some cases, entire peoples were deported: notably the Germans, the Chechens, Ingush and Balkars of the North Caucasus, the Kalmyks, and the Crimean Tatars. The legacy of these attempts to destroy whole peoples was their bitter and irrevocable hostility towards the Soviet Union, Communism, and Russians – a legacy which played a decisive role in the ultimate disintegration of the USSR. The first declarations of secession from the USSR came from the Baltic republics, the defection of the Ukrainians in 1991 completed the process, and the Chechens have provoked the most destructive of Russia's post-Soviet wars.

Chapter 7
The Soviet Union: triumph, decline, and fall

The Second World War and after

The Second World War exemplified in brutal fashion the advantages and disadvantages of Russia's geostrategic position. When Germany and its allies invaded in June 1941, the Red Army, destabilized by the terror and weakened by poor preparation, suffered terrible early losses, and retreated first of all to the outskirts of Moscow, then as far as the Volga at Stalingrad. The Germans occupied huge areas of the country, killing, enslaving, or deporting the inhabitants. Eventually, though, the strengths of Soviet totalitarian leadership reasserted themselves: the CPSU was able to prioritize the use of resources, shift industry to where it was more secure, and expand the production of armaments. 'Enemies' were now all too real, and Soviet citizens were powerfully motivated to fight them. The staunch fighting qualities of the Soviet soldier combined with popular Soviet-Russian patriotism, which even most non-Russians accepted when faced by German brutality. Recovery was gradual, but in the end, the greater size and resources of the Soviet Union, augmented by Allied aid, ensured victory.

As a result of that victory, the USSR gained an 'outer empire' in Central Europe and the Balkans, including part of Germany itself. It set about building Soviet-style socialism in its new dependencies, tolerating only minor deviations from the model to accommodate national distinctions. The methods by which pro-Soviet regimes were established and sustained alienated most of the local populations. They also alarmed the former Allies. The result was an 'iron curtain' running north–south through the middle of Europe. The traditional Russian–Western dichotomy now entrenched itself anew in the form of military alliances, the Warsaw Pact and NATO. The result was an uneasy peace, universally dubbed 'Cold War'.

The Second World War had changed Soviet society permanently, not necessarily to the benefit of the population. The ruling elite, both military and civilian, had proved their capacity to govern the country and achieve victory at a time of unprecedented danger. They had also become more independent of Stalin and more capable of defending their own interests. After 1945, terror was still applied, but on a much reduced scale compared with the 1930s. As for ordinary people, those who had survived were traumatized, most of them had lost family members, workplaces, and/or homes, and were more dependent on the ruling elite than ever before.

The official ideology had not changed much on the surface, but its inner content and the mentality of its audience had been transformed. The 'proletarian internationalism' of 1917 had now finally been replaced by a confident Russian-Soviet patriotism. 'Building communism' was still the official aim as post-war reconstruction got under way. But perpetual change was no longer acceptable, even to the younger generation. On the contrary, the Soviet Union was becoming a deeply conservative society, in which people struggled to acquire the minimum for a decent existence and then preserve it at all costs. Communism became an ever more ghostly aim, receding into an infinite future, whereas victory in 1945 was a definite and remarkable achievement. In subsequent decades, that victory, rather than the 1917 revolution, became the party's chief claim to popular support. Messianism was increasingly directed to a past event rather than a future one.

The USSR after Stalin

Stalin died in 1953. His legacy created huge difficulties for his successors. They knew that if another Stalin were allowed to emerge, they would probably be among his first victims. They acted quickly to bring the security police – now renamed the KGB – under the control of the Central Committee, so that it could no longer strike unrestrainedly against the *nomenklatura* elite.

More than that, however, they realized that mass terror was not in the long term a viable system of rule. But how could they keep control without it? Moreover, without revealing the truth about Stalin's crimes, how could they restrain terror in the future?

In the event, the new party first secretary, Khrushchev, decided on a limited revelation of the truth. At the 20th party congress in 1956, he denounced Stalin's repression of leading members of the *nomenklatura* elite and the deportations of nationalities. But he ignored the dekulakization and the famine of the 1930s – implying that these were entirely acceptable. Both what Khrushchev said and what he left unsaid were to become objects of heated controversy over the next decade, mostly in private and in the underground. What was crucial was that he had irrevocably destroyed the party's façade of unique and total rectitude. If it had made such terrible mistakes and committed such terrible crimes in the past, where was the guarantee it could not do so again? Many long-term prisoners were released from labour camps, but the rehabilitation of those unjustly arrested proceeded haltingly and eventually petered out. Stalin's ghost hung over everybody.

Khrushchev aimed to regain the population's trust by offering them growing material prosperity. He re-emphasized the party's millennial aims: at the 22nd party congress in 1961, he announced that by 1980 the Soviet Union would overtake the

USA in industrial output and thereby create 'the material prerequisites for communism'. Antagonistic social relationships had already come to an end, he claimed, and there was therefore no further need for the state as an organ of repression; it would 'fade away' and be replaced by the party as an agent of popular self-government. Khrushchev attempted to democratize the party by limiting the tenure of party secretaries at all levels and stipulating that they should be elected by secret ballot. This infuriated senior officials who since the death of Stalin had become accustomed to regarding their posts as more or less freehold entitlements. It was one reason why Khrushchev fell in 1964, dismissed by the Central Committee.

The new relationship between party and people required a reformed legal system, shorn of catch-all concepts like 'enemy of the people' and 'counter-revolutionary activity', which enabled prosecutors to incriminate anyone they chose. In principle, the new 'socialist legality' was to require genuine evidence of criminal activity to be produced in court before a conviction could be obtained. Judicial procedures were democratized by the introduction of 'comrade courts', consisting of ordinary citizens in the workplace or apartment block, empowered to reach a verdict and pronounce sentence on petty crimes. The idea was that society should become self-policing, at least for minor offences.

Stalin's successors attempted to increase agricultural production and make consumer goods available. Perhaps most important of all, they embarked on a huge programme of domestic construction, with the ultimate aim of providing each family with its own apartment. During the 1960s and 1970s, sufficient progress was made to turn most Soviet citizens into modest *de facto* property owners, with therefore a stake in preserving the system, whatever its faults. The Soviet welfare system also functioned well enough by the 1960s to give most citizens entitlements to education, child care, and health care, about whose defects they grumbled, without wishing to abolish them.

The collective strength of the ruling elite ensured that Soviet society became unyieldingly hierarchical. For most people, the way to get on in life was to elbow one's way upwards. The idea of a hierarchy of dwelling places may sound strange, but it was an integral part of Soviet life. For the supply of food, consumer goods, and social benefits in a society of scarcity, the best-provided city was Moscow; next came Leningrad and the capitals of the union republics; then towns with enterprises deemed 'of all-Union significance'; then other towns; and finally at the bottom of the ladder the villages. The aim of young people was to rise as far up this hierarchy as possible, using a mixture of educational qualifications and personal connections to obtain employment and a *propiska* (residence permit) in a higher-ranking location.

Those born in the villages tried to leave them. The long-term price of collectivization and neglect of agriculture was a poverty-stricken and demoralized countryside, populated mainly by women and elderly men who had not been able to escape. Young men found it easier to escape rural life than women, since military service enabled them to leave the village, acquire new skills, and obtain an urban *propiska*. Agricultural productivity was very low, as one could see in the empty shelves of grocers' shops. The Soviet state had to expend precious foreign currency importing grain in order to keep up the tacit 'social contract' with the urban workers: cheap food in return for low pay.

In the towns, the struggle for life chances became paramount. For many people, their employer was a vital resource person: if he could negotiate favourable deals with Gosplan, the supply of food, fuel, housing, *putevki* (paid holidays), and consumer goods was likely to be satisfactory for his employees. The benefits of the social security system were distributed at the workplace, through trade union branches. One might argue that every Soviet workplace was a 'primary collective', where the ostensible productive function was secondary to enabling people to conduct the normal and essential business of their lives *in spite of* the omnipresent pressure from the state.

Life inside the collective was fairly easy. One did not have to work too hard: pilfering, *tukhta* (padding the figures), and mutual cover-ups ensured that every employee could cope with life, no matter how deficient the collective's output. Since neither terror nor a normal market were available, it was impossible to eradicate these practices. On the other hand, talented or unusual people found life in the collective very difficult. To ensure its survival, the collective's members would band together to discipline or extrude individuals who might threaten its existence through non-conformity with prevailing social and political norms. In this way, collectives largely policed themselves: mutual surveillance remained one of their paramount functions.

In the struggle for life chances, another vital lubricator was *blat*. This was the unofficial mutual exchange of goods and services: one needed a patron with good access to official sources or a friend with a link to the shadow economy, where 'illegal' goods were obtainable. If a water pipe in the bathroom burst, then one needed someone to repair it urgently. The state repair system was usually too cumbersome to react speedily and effectively, so one would hastily ring round among friends and find a fitter who had access to the tools and lengths of pipe necessary to do the job. He would be diverting state property for his own personal profit, but at least he would perform the repair competently and in time to avoid major damage. In return, one would either offer some service or commodity, or pay him at a much higher rate than for state services.

Many forms of non-monetary exchange were mediated through personal relationships. If one needed to get one's son into a good school, one would work through acquaintances who knew the head teacher there. In return, one might be able to provide certain goods or services: a French perfume, an Italian suit, a Japanese tape recorder, or even just regular access to a good car repairer. In the process, one might actually form a good personal relationship. That was not necessary, but it would help to confirm and consolidate the exchange of goods and services. In this way, contrary to the theory of Hannah Arendt, who argued that totalitarianism 'atomized' society, new kinds of social bonds were generated, though totally unlike anything envisaged by the party.

This kind of social bonding became crucial in the field of science and culture. The USSR needed highly qualified scientists able to think independently and keep in touch with their foreign colleagues. Their institutes became islands of free thought and exchange of information not available to the ordinary population. Theatres, orchestras, publishing houses, and literary journals had their own tightly knit circles of creative personalities who chafed at party control and pervasive censorship. One of those journals, *Novy mir*, under its editor, Alexander Tvardovsky, himself a member of the CPSU Central Committee, managed to build on Khrushchev's revelations and tell more of the truth about the Soviet past. Alexander Solzhenitsyn's *A Day in the Life of Ivan Denisovich* (1962), which described honestly the routine of a Stalinist labour camp, broke a long-established taboo and aroused heartfelt reactions from its readers. Once again, literature was being forced to assume a civic, even a political, role as a kind of loyal opposition. In *Novy mir*, readers could follow in muffled form a debate which could not be articulated openly in the media.

The USSR was becoming more permeable. Information from the outside world was reaching it from its own 'outer empire', from Western visitors, and from Western short-wave radio stations. At its best, the Soviet education system produced enquiring minds, eager to absorb this information; and in their new private apartments, Soviet citizens could freely discuss with family and friends information and ideas excluded from the public media.

The result was to perpetuate the 19th-century dichotomy between Russia and 'the West', only now in a new form. Among free-thinking intellectuals reforming ideas took one of two paths. One could be called 'internationalist liberal', embodied in the person of the nuclear physicist Andrei Sakharov. He proposed that the Soviet Union should introduce genuine rule of law, legalize political opposition, reduce its armaments (especially nuclear), and fulfil the international commitments it had undertaken after the war. His position was strengthened by the Helsinki Final Act (1975), which finally confirmed the Soviet Union's post-1945 territorial gains, but also stipulated that all signatories should respect 'human rights and fundamental freedoms, including the freedom of thought, conscience, religion or belief'.

The other stream of underground oppositional thinking was Russian nationalist. As we have seen, Russian nationalism can take a mainly ethnic or mainly imperial form, and both trends existed, though the boundaries between them were blurred. What Russian nationalists could agree on was that Russians were a distinctively collectivist people, that unlike individualist, mercenary Westerners, they flourished by mutual support in adverse circumstances. Communist rule had weakened this inherited mutualism, they argued, and it had also reduced the population, blighted the natural environment, undermined the Orthodox Church, and destroyed peasant agriculture. Some, like Solzhenitsyn, thought the solution lay in withdrawing from great power politics, reducing the share of heavy industry in the economy, and returning to a simpler lifestyle based on organic agriculture and artisan production. Others, on the contrary, wanted to augment Russian imperial power by increasing heavy industrial and military production, and to strengthen the position of Russians as the state-bearing nationality by reducing the rights of non-Russians, especially Jews.

All these attitudes were reflected in the top echelons of the CPSU. The stronghold of the liberal Westernizing outlook was the

Central Committee's International Department. The Russianist outlook was strongest in the military and in the RSFSR (Russian republic) party apparatus. The party's official position was never clearly defined and wavered over time. On the whole, though, the leaders upheld internationalist Marxism-Leninism as the official ideology, while tolerating a simple-minded Russian imperial nationalism as a kind of 'working ideology' for everyday use. Obviously, this was not wholly acceptable in the party organizations of the non-Russian republics, but Leonid Brezhnev, CPSU General Secretary (1964–82), adopted a policy of 'stability of cadres' which offered their leaders the chance to devise their own local alternatives. They usually protected indigenous patron–client networks and tolerated a limited revival of local languages, histories, and cultures. As a result, by the 1970s, Russians living outside the RSFSR became gradually aware that being Russian was no longer an advantage in looking for education, jobs, or housing.

The end of the USSR

By the mid-1980s, the Soviet Union faced a serious internal crisis. It was failing to sustain the two major 'social contracts' on which its townsfolk depended: cheap food in return for low pay, and give and take between Russians and non-Russians.

The man who became CPSU General Secretary in March 1985, Mikhail Gorbachev, took over the views of the International Department. He had become convinced that the USSR was not increasing its security by accumulating nuclear and conventional weapons, but on the contrary undermining it by presenting to the outside world an 'enemy image', which provoked other powers to rearm against it. His 'new thinking' in foreign policy led him into a series of agreements with US President Reagan, in which both sides made deep cuts in their nuclear and conventional arsenals. At the United Nations, he explicitly renounced the 'primacy of the class struggle', which had hitherto been at the core of

Marxist-Leninist doctrine, and called for 'a world without violence and wars' and 'dialogue and cooperation for the sake of development and the preservation of civilisation'.

Internally, he launched a campaign against corruption and criminality in the *nomenklatura* elite. He encouraged *glasnost* (openness), so that ordinary citizens could denounce the misdeeds of their superiors. As his campaign advanced, he became convinced that his efforts were being resisted by what he called 'a managerial stratum, a ministerial and party apparatus which...does not want to give up its privileges'. The Chernobyl nuclear explosion of April 1986, whose seriousness officials tried to conceal from him, confirmed his suspicion. Within a few months, he had broadened *glasnost* into something more like freedom of speech. He also instituted *perestroika* (political reform), allowing oppositional political movements to disseminate their ideas, and eventually to take part in elections too. Newspapers began openly to criticize government policy. Sakharov was permitted to propagate his ideas freely, but so were nationalists, Russian and non-Russian. Solzhenitsyn published his three-volume *Gulag Archipelago*, which gave a fuller account than ever before of the terrible truth about Stalin's penal empire. A climax was reached in May 1989, when a new Congress of People's Deputies opened: one after another, speakers denounced the ruling class's abuses of power. It was televised live, and much of the population took time off work to watch, fascinated and appalled by the spectacle.

It soon became apparent, though, that the Soviet Union could not continue in anything like its present form if there were free speech and pluralist politics. As in the past, the bonds between the ruling class and the mass of people were too brittle to withstand serious strains. Besides, the 'outer empire' began to crumble even more quickly under the same pressures, until in 1989 the Berlin Wall fell, and a series of mostly peaceful revolutions brought non-Communist parties to power. The Warsaw Pact fell apart.

Inside the USSR, the strain fell first on the economy. Gorbachev launched a reform which legalized private economic enterprises. He intended that they should complement the planned state economy, but in practice they took advantage of shortages to offer higher prices to suppliers and charge customers more. As a result, they sucked goods out of the state economy; ordinary consumers could no longer afford everyday purchases. To make matters worse, the economic reforms also disrupted the informal practices by which people had received goods through their workplaces or personal networks. By 1990, it began to look as if routine food supplies might not reach the major cities.

Relations between the nationalities also suffered. The incongruity of simultaneously fostering and suppressing national consciousness now became obvious. *Glasnost* and political freedom brought festering enmities to the surface. Popular Fronts formed to express the ethnic grievances of the non-Russians. The Baltic republics, whose population had never fully accepted their 1940 incorporation into the USSR, began to demand autonomy, then full secession. Armenians and Azerbaijanis denounced each other, then actually went to war over Nagornyi Karabakh, a territory controlled by Azerbaijan where most of the population was Armenian. Abkhazia demanded secession from Georgia, while Georgia denounced Moscow for encouraging the Abkhazians. In April 1989, the Soviet army had to be called in to deal with massive demonstrations in Tbilisi. It killed at least twenty people, and a public enquiry was launched to investigate its actions.

These ethnic conflicts cast doubt on the viability of the Soviet Union as a federation of ethnically named republics. They also raised the question of the legality of turning the military against unarmed civilians. Commanders became nervous of using force to disperse rioters: they feared they might be held legally responsible for the resulting casualties.

These two developments came together in the Soviet Union's final crisis, which unexpectedly turned out to be a clash between Russia and the Soviet Union. Russians had long been aware that the non-Russian republics were becoming less hospitable homelands for them. In the late 1980s, their gradual exodus turned into a flood. Russians, who had taken it for granted that they were the dominant nationality and had not needed to defend their own identity, started to form their own organizations.

They had a problem, though: it was by no means clear what their national identity consisted of. There was still no coherent narrative of 'Russia'. Some Russians considered their country essentially an imperial state; others identified with its culture, religion, or ethnic traditions. Some Russian nationalists idolized Stalin as a great leader; others reviled him as the destroyer of the Russian peasantry and the Orthodox Church. Divided by their own heritage, Russian nationalists could not cooperate with one another, until Gorbachev's reforms threatened the actual break-up of the Soviet Union. By then it was too late.

Russia was not only a nation. It was also an institution, albeit a powerless one, within the USSR, the RSFSR. Gorbachev's reforms gave it real power for the first time, and Russian political movements sprang up, both liberal and nationalist-imperialist. At the liberal end, in March 1990 Democratic Russia won many seats in the RSFSR Congress of People's Deputies, and their spokesman, Boris Yeltsin, gained a perfect platform to denounce the CPSU and demand that Russia be allowed to run its own affairs. In June 1991, he was popularly elected President of the Russian Republic.

The nationalist-imperialists also formed their own political parties, which brought together environmental associations, cultural societies, military-patriotic organizations, and Russian 'international fronts' from the non-Russian republics. Their Patriotic Bloc fared poorly in the 1990 elections, but continued to warn of the dangers to which Gorbachev's peace-loving policy had exposed the Soviet Union. The reunification of Germany and its integration into NATO especially infuriated them: everything the Soviet Union had gained by its victory in the Second World War was, they claimed, now lost or jeopardized.

At the highest level of the CPSU, the nationalist-imperialists naturally had allies, who were becoming increasingly alarmed at Gorbachev's policies. When he tried to negotiate a new Union Treaty, which would radically redefine the relationships between the Union and the constituent republics, they decided to strike. On 19 August 1991, they formed an Emergency Committee, put Gorbachev under house arrest, and declared a state of emergency. They brought tanks into central Moscow to take the White House, home of the Russian parliament. They neglected, however, to arrest Yeltsin, who clambered on top of one of their tanks and denounced their coup, declaring it a 'crime against the legally elected authorities of the Russian Republic'.

13. Yeltsin interrupts Gorbachev at the podium, August 1991

This was the decisive moment. Uncertain which authority was legitimate, the army commanders declined to fire on civilians. Without their support, the Emergency Committee could not get a grip on the situation. Their coup collapsed, and within a few days, Yeltsin had outlawed the CPSU. Ukraine declared its independence, and its example was soon followed by most other republics.

The Soviet Union could not survive these blows. In December 1991, Yeltsin met with his Ukrainian and Belorussian counterparts and issued a declaration that 'the USSR, as a subject of international law and a geopolitical reality, has ceased to exist'. They announced they were setting up a Commonwealth of Independent States and invited the other Soviet republics to join them.

On the Kremlin roof, the hammer and sickle was taken down and replaced by the red-white-blue tricolour, which had been the flag of Russia's merchant navy before 1917. There was no double-headed eagle on it, which implied that Russia was renouncing its claim to empire. But what was to take its place? What was Russia now? The clash of symbols and narratives continued. The post-Soviet regime took a long time to decide what should be the new national flag, what should be the words of its national anthem, whether Lenin should remain in his Red Square mausoleum (he did), what its principal cities should be named (Leningrad became St Petersburg again, but the surrounding province remained *Leningradskaia oblast*), whether Nicholas II should be buried with full national honours (he was, in July 1998, but Yeltsin decided to attend only at the last moment, and the Patriarch stayed away). Even the country's official post-Soviet name, the Russian Federation (Russia), betrayed ambivalence over its status. In the new era of free speech and civil freedom, these issues were passionately debated in public.

The collapse of the Soviet Union was greeted by most of its nationalities as liberation. For Russians, it was more like deprivation – the loss of much of what they regarded as their homeland. Besides, the disappearance of the CPSU removed the cement that had enabled the state to function. Without it, the President and parliament were left facing one another without a mediator, and with no way of getting a grip on the regional strongmen or the new financial magnates. Yeltsin failed to persuade parliament to agree to a new constitution, and instead dissolved it in September 1993. Many of the deputies refused to accept his decision, declared his decree illegal, and deposed him as president. Paramilitary organizations came out to support them, and Yeltsin suddenly faced an armed rebellion in his capital city. He responded by summoning tanks to storm the White House. This time, Pavel Grachev, the Defence Minister, agreed, but insisted that Yeltsin sign a written statement taking responsibility for the bloodshed.

This confrontation finally ended the Soviet era, but it also exposed the continuing weakness of the Russian state, its failure even to ensure its own monopoly of violence. That failure continued to be in evidence in the following two decades. Without the CPSU, the component cells of a state were left floundering, looking for a new legal and symbolic framework which would impart structure and purpose.

In this vacuum of legitimate authority, a full-scale economic reform finally took place. Launched by a bright and arrogant group of young economists, devotees of the radical free-market 'Washington consensus', it soon provided yet another example of a Western panacea which proved disastrous when applied to Russia. They launched a mass programme of privatization and freeing of prices, which provoked hyper-inflation and transferred most productive resources into the hands of enterprising and ruthless businessmen – the 'oligarchs'. The state, meanwhile, was left impoverished and without a reliable method of levying taxes: it could not even pay schoolteachers and pensioners on time. Unable to rely on the police to keep order, firms employed their own private security firms or paid money to protection gangs.

There was now little to prevent non-Russian autonomous republics within Russia declaring their own secession. In the event, only one did so, Chechnia, but the consequences were destructive and far-reaching. After negotiating for three years, Yeltsin decided in 1994 to restore authority by sending in the Russian army. It suffered a series of humiliating reverses and eventually had to withdraw. In 1999, it invaded again, and after a long and indecisive campaign, left Chechnia in the hands of a local warlord under uncertain Kremlin control. The Chechen experience revealed brutally Russia's weakness and deepened the corruption and violence prevalent in both military and civilian leadership.

Under Yeltsin in the 1990s, then, oligarchs, provincial governors, and ethnic separatists each built their own sub-state networks, controlling access to capital and coercive resources. Ordinary people became more dependent than ever before on their bosses and other local magnates for the routine facilities of life: housing, food, transport, health care, recreation, and the education of their children, even sometimes for their physical safety. Most Western commentators on the early post-Soviet years wrote as if the choice for Russia was between authoritarianism and democracy. In actual fact, the real issue was whether Russia was going to have an effective state at all. If not, its population would have to place its trust in such lower-level leaders and institutions as could protect them and provide them with life's necessities.

After he became President in 2000, Vladimir Putin in some respects strengthened the state, which he referred to as the 'power vertical'. In ruthless manner, he brought Chechnia back under nominal Russian control. He simplified taxes, to make them easier to understand and harder to evade; they were also centralized, to facilitate redistribution and alleviate the glaring disparity between richer and poorer regions. Rising oil and gas prices enabled the government to pay schoolteachers and pensioners on time.

Like earlier Russian rulers, however, Putin strengthened the state largely through the manipulation of personalized networks. He ended the election of provincial governors and tightened Kremlin control over them. He made the Duma, the post-1993 parliament, more compliant, and sponsored the largest party, United Russia, as a permanent government majority inside it. In the interests of what he called 'information security', he brought most of the media, especially television, under tight supervision. He came to an understanding with the oligarchs, under which the dubious sources of their wealth would not be investigated, provided they kept out of politics. When one of them, Mikhail Khodorkovsky, stepped out of line by financing Duma deputies, he was arrested and charged with fraud, tax evasion, and embezzlement. This was not only an economic move: as well as an oligarch, Khodorkovsky was also a potential presidential candidate. He had proposed strengthening the rule of law, adopting a more open and pluralist style of politics, and a more transparent system of corporate governance, compatible with international standards of financial probity. After his arrest, his successful oil firm, Yukos, passed into the hands of senior government officials, who thus became oligarchs themselves. Robber barons had moved into the highest echelons of the state.

Putin, and his rather shadowy successor, Dmitry Medvedev, have fallen well short of consolidating the state by grounding it in popular trust or stable institutions. Without the rule of law or strong political parties, authoritarian rule means in practice that the wealth of society is the object of competition between powerful patron–client cliques, who are able to operate unchallenged and in the obscurity provided by media deference and censorship. Russian government is still at the mercy of the same cliques, now at the very heart of the state; it has become more corrupt under Putin. Meanwhile, popular unrest is expressed in spontaneous demonstrations and strikes, protesting against local abuses of power but unable to affect the political system as a whole.

Conclusion

In the 16th century, Muscovy improvised an authority structure which would enable it to cope with the challenges it faced both from the steppe and from European great powers. The resulting Russian Empire was remarkably successful: it became the largest territorial state on earth and outlasted most of its rivals. It offered its population basic physical security, modest but assured access to resources, and membership of stable communities. It also proved successful on the whole at integrating non-Russian peoples. On the other hand, the state's overweening exercise of authority, its dependence on wilful and often corrupt agents, and the general weakness of law and institutions impeded economic development, enfeebled the link between elites and masses, and generated bitter resentments which sporadically burst forth in rebellion. Discontent was intensified in the late 19th and early 20th centuries by the penetration of European ideas into ever broader strata of the population.

The First World War nearly destroyed Russia, but it revived for a time as the Soviet Union, and even after the latter's collapse, it survives in reduced form. The authoritarian and personalized political structure which brought it success in the past is, however, ill-suited to the entirely different challenges Russia faces today, of adjusting to a global high-tech economy and an increasingly interdependent world in which nuclear weapons have made war between major powers virtually impossible.

Today, moreover, Russians are better educated than in the past, and they have incomparably more experience of life outside their own country, especially in Europe and North America. The age-old justification of authoritarianism – that the country faces powerful external threats – is no longer persuasive. The gap between rulers and ruled is widening once more. Russia is one of the world's great survivors, and it will probably cope in its own way with these challenges. How it will do so is at the moment impossible to say.

Further reading

General

The themes of this book are treated at greater length in Geoffrey
    Hosking, *Russia and the Russians*, 2nd edn. (2011).
Philip Longworth, *Russia's Empires: Their Rise and Fall from
    Prehistory to Putin* (2005) is a lively and up-to-date account of
    Russia's various imperial reincarnations.
On the difficulty of building a Russian nation within a Russian
    empire, see Vera Tolz, *Russia: Inventing a Nation* (2001).
Timothy Snyder, *The Reconstruction of Nations: Poland, Ukraine,
    Lithuania, Belarus, 1569–1999* (2003) tells an important story
    about the collision of national projects on Russia's western border.
Marshall Poe, *The Russian Moment in World History* (2003) briefly
    presents an important thesis about Russia's evolution as a state.

Chapter 1

Simon Franklin and Jonathan Shepard, *The Emergence of Rus,
    750–1200* (1996) is an excellent scholarly introduction to its
    subject.
Janet Martin, *Medieval Russia, 980–1584* (1995).
Serge A. Zenkovsky (ed.), *Medieval Russia's Epics, Chronicles and
    Tales* (1974).
David Morgan, *The Mongols* (1986).
Robert O. Crummey, *The Formation of Muscovy, 1304–1613* (1987).

Chapter 2

Donald Ostrowski, *Muscovy and the Mongols: Cross-Cultural Influences on the Steppe Frontier* (1998) stresses the Mongol heritage in Muscovy.

Nancy Shields Kollmann, *By Honor Bound: State and Society in Early Modern Russia* (1999).

Isabel de Madariaga, *Ivan the Terrible* (2005), a good recent scholarly biography.

Robert Frost, *The Northern Wars, 1558–1721* (2000) offers the European background to Muscovy's evolution into the Russian Empire.

Brian L. Davies, *Warfare, State and Society on the Black Sea Steppe, 1500–1700* (2007) does the same for the steppe frontier.

Philip Longworth, *The Cossacks* (1969).

Chapter 3

John LeDonne, *The Russian Empire and the World, 1700–1917: The Geopolitics of Expansion and Containment* (1997) is not an easy read, but a valuable account of Imperial Russia's geopolitical situation.

William Fuller, *Strategy and Power in Russia, 1600–1914* (1992), similar, with more emphasis on military matters.

Iver B. Neumann, *Russia and the Idea of Europe: A Study in Identity and International Relations* (1996).

Lindsey Hughes, *Russia in the Age of Peter the Great* (1998) is now the standard work on Peter the Great.

Isabel de Madariaga, *Russia in the Age of Catherine the Great* (2002) does the same for Catherine the Great.

Elise Kimerling Wirtschafter, *Russia's Age of Serfdom, 1649–1861* (2008).

Dominic Lieven, *Russia against Napoleon: The Battle for Europe, 1807–1814* (2009), not only the best book on its subject, but also an excellent summary of Imperial Russia's military organization.

Janet Hartley, *Alexander I* (1994) is a good biography and assessment.

Chapter 4

Dominic Lieven, *Empire: The Russian Empire and Its Rivals* (2000) makes an illuminating comparison between Russia and other major empires.

Andreas Kappeler, *The Russian Empire: A Multiethnic History* (2001) is the best account of the development of the non-Russian peoples and their relationship with the imperial state.

Geoffrey Hosking, *Russia: People and Empire* (1997) endeavours to do the same for the Russians.

Chapter 5

Ben Eklof, John Bushnell, and Larissa Sakharova (eds.), *Russia's Great Reforms, 1855–1881* (1994).

Dominic Lieven, *Nicholas II: Emperor of all the Russias* (1993).

Hans Rogger, *Russia in the Age of Modernisation and Revolution, 1881–1917* (1983).

Nicholas Rzhevsky (ed.), *The Cambridge Companion to Modern Russian Culture* (1998).

Peter Gatrell, *The Tsarist Economy, 1850–1917* (1986).

S. A. Smith, *The Russian Revolution: A Very Short Introduction* (2002) offers well what its title suggests.

The second half of Orlando Figes, *A People's Tragedy: The Russian Revolution, 1891–1924* (1996) provides a good longer narrative of 1917–24.

John L. H. Keep, *The Russian Revolution: A Study in Mass Mobilization* (1976) does well what its subtitle promises.

Chapter 6

For a general history of the Soviet Union, see Geoffrey Hosking, *A History of the Soviet Union* (1992); Ronald Suny, *The Soviet Experiment: Russia, the USSR and the Successor States* (1998); Stephen Lovell, *The Soviet Union: A Very Short Introduction* (2009).

Robert Service, *Lenin: A Political Biography* (3 vols, 1985–95) is the best biography of Lenin. Those who want a shorter account will find Adam Ulam, *Lenin and the Bolsheviks* (1969) still very useful.

Oleg V. Khlevniuk, *Master of the House: Stalin and His Inner Circle* (2009) is the best-informed account of Stalin's terror.

Jörg Baberowski, *Der rote Terror: die Geschichte des Stalinismus* (2003).

Sheila Fitzpatrick, *Stalin's Peasants: Resistance and Survival in the Russian Village after Collectivization* (1994); and *Everyday*

Stalinism: Ordinary Life in Extraordinary Times: Soviet Russia in the 1930s (1999).

Alexander Werth, *Russia at War, 1941–1945* (1964): lively reportage by a journalist on the Soviet home front.

John Barber and Mark Harrison, *The Soviet Home Front, 1941–1945: A Social and Economic History of the USSR in World War II* (1991).

Catherine Merridale, *Ivan's War: The Red Army, 1939–45* (2005), and her *Night of Stone: Death and Memory in Russia* (2000) both throw light on the personal ordeal of ordinary Russians, civilian and military.

Chapter 7

The postwar USSR has yet to receive full scholarly treatment, but John Keep, *Last of the Empires: A History of the Soviet Union, 1945–1991* (1995), and Stephen Lovell, *The Shadow of War: Russia and the USSR, 1941 to the Present* (2010) are two excellent general studies.

On the most important leaders, see William Taubman, *Khrushchev: The Man and His Era* (2003), and Archie Brown, *The Gorbachev Factor* (2003).

John Dunlop, *The Rise of Russia and the Fall of the Soviet Empire* (1995).

Timothy J. Colton, *Yeltsin: A Life* (2008).

Lilia Shevtsova, *Russia – Lost in Transition: The Yeltsin and Putin Years* (2007).

Simon Pirani, *Change in Putin's Russia: Power, Money and People* (2010).

Chronology

Principal grand princes and tsars

Kiev

978–1015	Vladimir
1019–54	Iaroslav the Wise
1113–25	Vladimir Monomakh

Novgorod

1236–63	Alexander Nevskii

Moscow

c. 1276–1303	Daniil
1325–41	Ivan I (Kalita)
1359–89	Dmitrii Donskoi
1462–1505	Ivan III
1505–33	Vasilii III
1533–84	Ivan IV (the Terrible)
1584–98	Fedor I
1598–1605	Boris Godunov
1604–13	Time of Troubles
1613–45	Mikhail
1645–76	Aleksei

St Petersburg

1682–1725	(till 1696 jointly with Ivan V) Peter I (the Great)
1727–30	Peter II
1730–40	Anna
1741–61	Elizabeth
1761–2	Peter III
1762–96	Catherine II (the Great)
1796–1801	Paul
1801–25	Alexander I
1825–55	Nicholas I
1855–81	Alexander II
1881–94	Alexander III
1894–1917	Nicholas II

Principal Soviet leaders

1917–24	Vladimir Lenin (as Prime Minister)
1922–53	Joseph Stalin (as Party General Secretary)
1953–64	Nikita Khrushchev (as Party First Secretary)
1964–82	Leonid Brezhnev (as Party General Secretary)
1985–91	Mikhail Gorbachev (as Party General Secretary)

Main events

988	Kievan Rus accepts Christianity
1054	Split between Byzantine and Roman churches
1237–42	Mongol armies conquer most of Rus
1240–2	Alexander Nevskii defeats Swedes and Teutonic Knights
1326	Kiev Metropolitanate transferred to Moscow
1362	Battle of Blue Waters
1380	Battle of Kulikovo
1438–9	Council of Ferrara-Florence
1453	Byzantine falls to the Ottoman Turks
1478	Novgorod acknowledges Muscovite sovereignty

1480	Muscovy ceases to acknowledge sovereignty of Golden Horde
1480s–90s	Golden Horde breaks up
1547	Ivan IV is crowned Tsar
1550	*Sudebnik* (Law Code)
1552	Conquest and annexation of Kazan
1556	Conquest and annexation of Astrakhan
1556	Decree on Service
1558–82	Livonian War
1564–72	Creation of *oprichnina*
1571	Crimean Tatars sack Moscow
1589	Creation of Moscow Patriarchate
1613	*Zemskii sobor* elects Mikhail Romanov Tsar
1648	Dnieper Cossack rebellion against Poland
1649	*Ulozhenie* (Law Code)
1652–8	Nikon as Patriarch
1654	Annexation of Dnieper Cossack Hetmanate (Ukraine)
1666–7	Church Council anathematizes the Old Belief
1667–71	Rising of Stenka Razin
1703	Establishment of new capital: St Petersburg
1705	Establishment of permanent standing army
1709	Victory over Sweden at Poltava
1721	Abolition of Patriarchate
1721	Annexation of Baltic provinces
1722	Institution of Table of Ranks
1723	Introduction of poll tax
1726	Establishment of Russian Academy of Sciences
1730	Empress Anna rejects 'Conditions'
1732	Foundation of Cadet Corps
1755	Establishment of Moscow University
1756–63	Seven Years War
1762	Emancipation of *dvorianstvo* from state service

1767–8	Law Code Commission
1768–74	War with Ottoman Empire
1772, 1793, 1795	Partitions of Poland
1773–5	Pugachev rising
1791	Establishment of Jewish Pale of Settlement
1801	Annexation of Georgia
1805–15	Wars against Napoleon
1812	French invasion of Russia
1825	Decembrist revolt
1830–1	Polish rising
1833	Pushkin completes *The Bronze Horseman*
1842	Publication of Gogol's *Dead Souls*
1853–6	Crimean War
1859	Capture of Shamil
1861	Emancipation of serfs
1863–4	Polish rising
1864–6	Publication of Dostoevsky's *Notes from Underground* and *Crime and Punishment*
1865–76	Conquest of Kokand, Khiva, and Bukhara
1869	Publication of Tolstoy's *War and Peace*
1873–4	Populists' 'going to the people'
1874, 1880	First performances of Mussorgsky's *Boris Godunov* and *Khovanshchina*
1874	Introduction of universal male military service
1877–8	War against Ottoman Empire
1879	Formation of *Narodnaia volia*
1881	Assassination of Alexander II
1882	Anti-Jewish May Laws
1898	Formation of Social Democratic Workers' Party
1899	Imperial Manifesto on Finland
1901	Formation of Socialist Revolutionary Party
1903	SD Party splits into Bolsheviks and Mensheviks

1903	Completion of Trans-Siberian Railway
1904–5	Russo-Japanese War
1905–6	First Russian Revolution
October 1905	October Manifesto
April 1906	Formation of State Duma
November 1906	Stolypin's agrarian reform
June 1907	Revision of Duma electoral law
1911	Assassination of Stolypin
1913	First performance of Stravinsky's *Rite of Spring*
August 1914	Outbreak of First World War
1915	Loss of Poland
February–March 1917	February Revolution; formation of Provisional Government and soviets
October 1917	October Revolution
January 1918	Dissolution of Constituent Assembly
March 1918	Treaty of Brest-Litovsk; Russia withdraws from the war
1922	Formation of USSR
1922	Stalin becomes General Secretary of the Communist Party
January 1924	Death of Lenin
1928	Beginning of First Five Year Plan
1929	Launch of dekulakization and collectivization of agriculture
1932	Creation of Union of Soviet Writers
1932	Introduction of internal passports and *propiska*
1932–4	Widespread famine
1937–8	Height of Stalin's terror
August 1939	Nazi-Soviet Pact
September 1939	Red Army occupies eastern Poland (western Ukraine and Belorussia)
March–May 1940	Katyn mass murder of Poles
June 1940	Annexation of Baltic states

June 1941	Germany invades USSR
August 1942–February 1943	Battle of Stalingrad
1944	Deportation of Caucasian and other peoples
May 1945	Germany surrenders to USSR
1949	Formation of NATO
March 1953	Death of Stalin
1955	Formation of Warsaw Pact
February 1956	20th Party Congress; Khrushchev's 'secret speech'
1962	Publication of Solzhenitsyn's *A Day in the Life of Ivan Denisovich*
October 1964	Fall of Khrushchev; Brezhnev becomes party leader
1975	Helsinki Final Act
March 1985	Gorbachev becomes General Secretary of CPSU
April 1986	Chernobyl nuclear explosion
1988	Popular Fronts formed in Baltic and elsewhere; beginning of Armenian-Azerbaijani conflict
April 1989	Violent suppression of Tbilisi demonstrations
May 1989	Congress of People's Deputies in Moscow
November 1989	Fall of Berlin Wall
March 1990	Non-Communist parties legalized
March 1990	Democratic Russia wins seats in RSFSR legislature
March 1990	Lithuania secedes from USSR (followed by Latvia and Estonia)
June 1990	Formation of Russian Communist Party
April 1991	Georgia secedes from USSR
June 1991	Yeltsin elected as President of Russia

August 1991	Emergency Committee coup
December 1991	Dissolution of USSR
1992	Privatization law
September–October 1993	Conflict between Yeltsin and Russian parliament
December 1993	Creation of State Duma
December 1994	Russian army invades Chechnia
September 1999	Start of Second Chechen War
December 1999	Yeltsin resigns as President
March 2000	Putin is elected as President
October 2003	Arrest of Khodorkovsky
March 2008	Medvedev is elected as President

Glossary

artel	workers' cooperative
Autonomous Republic	in the Soviet administrative hierarchy: a republic one level below the 15 Union Republics
blat	informal exchange of goods and/or services
boyars	leading warriors
Cheka	Extraordinary Commission for Combating Counter-Revolution and Sabotage; security police (1917–22)
CPSU	Communist Party of the Soviet Union
druzhina	squad of armed henchmen
dvorianstvo	nobility
glasnost	openness, transparency
grazhdanstvennost	civic consciousness or spirit
guberniia	province
Gulag	NKVD department which ran prisons and labour camps; the network of prisons and labour camps
iarlyk	Mongol licence to rule
intelligentsia	radical intellectuals
KGB	Committee of State Security; security police (1954–91)

kolkhoz	collective farm
kommunalka	communal apartment
korenizatsiia	indigenization: the policy of promoting non-Russian institutions and cultures
kormlenie	'feeding': support in kind for a ruler's local representative
krugovaia poruka	joint responsibility
lavra	a leading monastery
likbez	liquidation of illiteracy
metropolitan	bishop of a leading city
mir	self-governing local community
narod	people, ethnos
narodnik	populist
NKVD	People's Commissariat of Internal Affairs; security police (1934–46)
nomenklatura	Communist Party appointments system; the ruling class thus generated
obshchestvennost	public opinion; society, as opposed to the state
obshchina	village community
perestroika	political reform (under Gorbachev)
pomeshchik	holder of a *pomestie*
pomestie	landed estate granted in return for service
pravda	truth, justice
propiska	residence permit
putevki	paid holidays
RSFSR	Russian Soviet Federated Socialist Republic (much the largest of the 15 Union Republics of the USSR)
Rus	the medieval term for the lands of the East Slavs; *Rossiia* is a Latin translation of it, used from the 17th century
skit	hermitage

skomorokhi	strolling players
sobornost	spirit of community
soviet	originally: workers' council
starosta	elder
tariqat	Sufi brotherhoods
tukhta	artificially inflating production figures
uezd	district
ulus	a nomadic people and its territory in the Mongol Empire
USSR	Union of Soviet Socialist Republics, or Soviet Union, consisting of 15 Union Republics
veche	urban assembly
volost	township (peasant institution)
votchina	hereditary estate
zemliachestvo	association of workers from the same province
zemstvo	elected local government assembly
znamenny	traditional Russian liturgical chant

Index

THE SOVIET UNION
A Very Short Introduction
Stephen Lovell

Almost twenty years after the Soviet Unions' end, what are we to make of its existence? Was it a heroic experiment, an unmitigated disaster, or a viable if flawed response to the modern world? Taking a fresh approach to the study of the Soviet Union, this Very Short Introduction blends political history with an investigation into the society and culture at the time. Stephen Lovell examines aspects of patriotism, political violence, poverty, and ideology; and provides answers to some of the big questions about the Soviet experience.

Expand your collection of
VERY SHORT INTRODUCTIONS